LONDON RECORD SOCIETY
PUBLICATIONS

VOLUME XXXVII

General Editor for this volume: V.A. Harding

UNPUBLISHED LONDON DIARIES

A Checklist of unpublished diaries by Londoners and visitors
with a Select Bibliography of published diaries

COMPILED BY

HEATHER CREATON

LONDON RECORD SOCIETY
2003

Dedicated to
the happy memory of my husband, Peter Brooke

Typeset and printed by
Q3 Print Project Management, Loughborough, Leicestershire

CONTENTS

ABBREVIATIONS USED IN
THE LIST OF DIARIES

ANZAC	Australian and New Zealand Army Corps
ARP	Air Raid Precautions
Bart	baronet
c.	*circa*
City	City of London
Coll	college
Colln	Collection
D-Day	invasion of France (1944)
HM	His/Her Majesty's
LCC	London County Council
Middx	Middlesex
mf	microfilm
MP	Member of Parliament
PRO	Public Record Office
RAAF	Royal Australian Air Force
RAF	Royal Air Force
RAMC	Royal Army Medical Corps
RN	Royal Navy
RNVR	Royal Naval Volunteer Reserve
RSA	Royal Society of Arts
V1	flying bomb
V2	rocket weapon
VAD	Voluntary Aid Detachment (nurses)
VE	victory in Europe celebrations
VJ	victory in Japan celebrations
WAAC	Women's Army Auxiliary Corps
WAAF	Women's Auxiliary Air Force
WRNS	Women's Royal Naval Service
WVS	Women's Voluntary Service

ILLUSTRATIONS

INTRODUCTION

The London Record Society was founded to stimulate interest in historical documents relating to London by publishing both scholarly editions of important texts and lists of relevant primary sources. The present volume falls within the latter category. It contains a list of eight hundred and eighty-three unpublished diaries, with an index to their writers and to their general subject content. A second checklist of two hundred and forty-four published diaries follows, indexed by writer and editor. The compilation work was undertaken over several years, as part of the editor's duties at the Centre for Metropolitan History, a section of the University of London's Institute of Historical Research. The checklist of manuscripts endeavours to provide general guidance concerning the contents of each diary, but space does not permit many quotations from the diaries within the list itself. Instead, this introduction will give some indication of the type of material to be found in the original documents. This is both varied and rewarding for the historian.

In a city of London's complexity and size, it can be difficult to pinpoint the experience of the individual at a specific period. Diaries, however, represent a valuable approach into this elusive world, presenting unique snapshots of life in the city at different times and at varying social levels. Diarists may concentrate on great events or on the comparative trivia of their everyday round, but they all convey some genuine flavour of London life that is hard to find in other sources. Diaries of any period can make gripping reading, reflecting the writer's personality as well as the atmosphere of his times. Events may unfold inexorably day by day, their likely outcome often clearer to the modern reader than to the writer, who was probably less aware of an emerging pattern. Such diaries represent core material for the biographer, but they can be valuable to any historian. The minutiae of personal routines may yield detailed information about the practicalities of daily life too trivial to mention in more 'serious' writing, as well as giving insights into attitudes, expectations and behaviour in different social milieux. High politics to housework, childbirth to deathbeds, burglaries to bowel movements, all are recorded by diarists in this checklist. The editor hopes that it will point all those interested in London history to the great range of underused, as yet unpublished diary material available in collections throughout this country and abroad.

Compiling the checklist

Finding the diaries for this checklist was an intriguing, rewarding and sometimes frustrating process. Like most similar projects, it took longer than originally planned. Valuable diaries are sure to have been missed, but one cannot search for ever. If readers of this collection will be kind enough to suggest additions and corrections, the editor will gladly note them for a supplement.

Bibliographies of diaries provided the starting point for this compilation. William Matthew's *British Diaries* (1950), J S Batts's *British Manuscript Diaries of the Nineteenth Century* (1976), C A Huff's *British Women's Diaries* (1985) and others noted in the bibliography all contain relevant items. Some of these titles are now quite old, and the diary locations they listed have often changed, especially if the manuscripts were then in private hands. Many of these are now on deposit in record offices, but others have effectively disappeared. The National Register of Archives' online indexes have been indispensable (hmc.gov.uk/nra) as have the detailed lists in their searchroom. Repository catalogues, whether paper or online, in the UK and abroad, have also yielded many references, and in passing the editor became a connoisseur of terse archival descriptions. Who can resist the weary tone of 'Journal of several shooting parties over various Scottish moors' or the more alluring 'Travel journal of a young governess from Rochester to Germany ... on the way her ship is captured by French privateers'?

As 'diary' or 'journal' is not usually an archival search term, it is necessary to look among groups of personal papers, whether of families or individuals, in quest of these items. Sometimes they are catalogued in the 'miscellaneous' category, always a fascinating assortment of oddments and unexpected treasures in repository lists. Is there a difference between diaries and journals? When William Matthews, the doyen of diary bibliographers, was starting his work, he attempted to differentiate between the two. He soon admitted defeat, and the checklist follows his distinguished lead in this matter. Journals are diaries for present purposes, their writers used the terms interchangeably.

The format of the diaries examined varied considerably. Some were written in notebooks, ruled or unruled, occasionally bound up later. Printed diaries came on the market in the late eighteenth century. Many diarists adopted them and tailored their daily entry to fit the space provided. Some people preferred the freedom of the open page, writing long entries for some days and much shorter ones for others. Additional evidence can often be gathered from the diarist's choice of format, page layout and regular abbreviations. Handwriting too – varying with tiredness, emotional state, illness and increasing age – can add to the overall impression of the writer's personality and character. Typescript diaries, and those on computer disk, give fewer of these extra clues. Some diarists record their daily doings on audio tape – the politician Tony Benn is a prime example.

The editor looked for personal diaries containing material about London, whether by residents or a visitor, the sort of diaries that convey a flavour of London life. The entries were written up daily, or within a short time of the events they describe, while still fresh and immediate in the writer's mind. Memoirs written later have been excluded. It was not possible to examine nearly nine hundred diaries personally, though the editor saw many of those held by libraries and record offices in the London area. For the rest, she relied on catalogues and lists that vary in the quantity of detail provided. It can be hard to tell from a repository list how much time a non-resident diarist actually spent in the capital. Among the papers of county families, for example, there are many diaries that cover life at the country house and foreign travel, but also record regular visits to London for the 'season'. In other cases a provincial diarist may make frequent visits to the capital for business or legal meetings, medical treatment, family events or merely for shopping. The editor has tried to indicate the dates of the London visits within the wider coverage.

Purely 'work' diaries have not been included – like those of the blacksmith Edward Keyte (WCA Acc 701), or Alfred Kisch, Medical Officer to the Jews' Orphan Asylum, (Wellcome MS 3116) – interesting though they are, because the project has concentrated on personal, social material. It was tempting to make an exception here and there – a purely farming diary from Ruislip in 1829 (LMA Acc 538/1/8/11) contains the laconic but intriguing entry 'The Bald Horse went Mad and was shot by Wm Larch' – but its inclusion could not be justified on that alone. There is work content in many of the diaries, of course – like the cabinet-maker Job Knight (**200**): 'Rose in better health & spirits after breakfasting at home took my usual walk to St Paul's, my drawing approved by the Junior partner…', but interspersed with domestic and social affairs. Wholly spiritual diaries are also excluded, as well as very brief engagement diaries that only note dentists' appointments and the like. Just occasionally, this type can disgorge intriguing snippets such as this hint of an uncomfortable Christmas found in an almost empty, and anonymous, diary for 1939 (MoL Almanacks/D2): '26 Dec. 1938 Rushed to Hospital with sharp bone in my throat'. 27 Dec. 'X-rayed. Bone out', but not enough to warrant an entry in the list.

For checklist purposes, London encompasses what is now thought of as 'Greater London', thereby admitting diarists such as Philadelphia Lee (**114**) of Totteridge, and Rebecca Shaen (**141**) of Walthamstow, then comparatively rural, as well as central Londoners. Some of the diarists living on the outskirts of London regularly came in to the centre for work and pleasure. H Longman (**275**) of Sheepcote Farm, Harrow, nicely combined country and city interests one day in 1834: 'Horses at plough. Went to see the ruins of the Houses of Parliament. Took two pigs to Mr Sommers…'

All bibliographical projects relating to London soon encounter the same basic problem. London has been the nation's capital for many centuries. Much that happens there relates to national, rather than London history. It can be difficult, for example, to extricate political and financial matters from personal and local material, especially in the diaries of statesmen, industrialists and financiers. Diaries that are entirely political or parliamentary have been excluded, though the distinction is sometimes hard to make. If they definitely contain some social, domestic and personal content – like those of Sir John Hobhouse (**169**), or Sir James Stephen (**330**), they have been included.

The diarists

There are many psychological theories about diary-keeping. Some see diarists as self-centred egoists whose own activities assume supreme importance. Others interpret the diary as a recurring 'cry for help' in an indifferent or hostile world. More prosaically, diarists often write regular entries simply as a defence against a fallible memory. There are probably as many reasons for diary-keeping as there are diary-writers. Occasionally the diarist will specify why he or she has decided to begin. William Cooper (**105**), an eighteenth century medical student, noted '...the intention of this Diary is as a mirror to shew me my transactions, so that I may be able to improve my Time to the greatest advantage...'. Canon Hall (**491**) sets out to make a record of his life 'for the benefit or amusement of my children'. The costume historian, John Nevinson (**636**) began writing at school, in 1923, explaining that the diary would be a 'safety-valve to my passing emotions', and vowing to re-read it in the future 'when I shall be able to form a better opinion of the past'. He stuck to that resolution, and his later comments, annotating his diaries in 1943 and again in 1973, make an interesting contrast. Whatever the original reason for starting a diary, once the habit is established many writers plough on indefinitely. The checklist contains some long-running examples. Norris Purslow (**21**) wrote from 1690 to 1737, John Dawson (**39**) from 1722 to 1763. Robert Ramsay's diary (**495**) spanned 1869–1951 – though he did not reach London until 1882 – and Anthony Heap (**640**) kept his from 1928 to 1985, Alan Withington (**646**) from 1931–98.

The diary habit does not 'take' in all cases. There are many apparently short-lived diaries in the checklist, though possibly earlier and later volumes have been lost. John Pritt Harley (**397**) was clearly a creature of habit. It seems unlikely that he embarked on diary-keeping for the first time at the age of seventy, but his volume for 1854 is the only one known to survive. In other cases the new diarist simply loses impetus, though most last longer than Sarah Mence (Wigan AS EHC 44) who gave up after one page in 1840. This waning of enthusiasm is particularly noticeable a century later, when a considerable number of people began a diary in 1939 to record the momentous outbreak of the Second World War. Some were writing at the suggestion of the Mass-Observation organisation, others wrote independently, but a large proportion of them appear to have become bored during the 'phoney war' and abandoned the diary habit for lack of dramatic developments to write about. Ironically, those who persevered are of particular interest to the modern reader precisely because they wrote about the ordinary difficulties of daily life as the war progressed – lack of sleep because of air raids, reactions to transport disruption, evacuation, rationing, refugees, overseas troops – rather than regurgitating the progress of the military campaign as reported in their daily newspapers.

The proportion of London residents to visitors in this checklist is roughly 8:2. The residents vary widely. Some are Londoners born and bred, like Georgiana Keate (**122**) and Andrew Tait (**539**), others have migrated to London at some stage in life, like Samuel Kevan (**136**) who originally came from Wigtown. The visitors are similarly varied. There are regular visitors, who come to see relations, like George Pegler (**353**) or to do the season, like the Marchioness of Huntly (**316**). There are the once-in-a-lifetime visitors like Betsy Barrett (**224**) in 1824, who did not expect to return: 'Breakfasted and was quite out of spirits and left London at two in the afternoon never I fear to revisite again'.

Big events, like the Great Exhibition in 1851, brought more once-in-a-lifetime visitors. Emigrants from other parts of the country often started their adventurous journey with a stay in London before embarking for Canada, Australia or New Zealand. Services personnel in both World Wars, wherever they were stationed in the UK, liked to spend their leave in London, their diaries mixing service life with details of their amusements while off duty in town. Among them were many of the overseas visitors listed in the index, a category making up 40 per cent of the total of visitors' diaries in the checklist. Their insights into London life can be of especial interest. Outsiders often describe what London residents thought too commonplace for comment, like the gloom of a London Sunday experienced by the Swedish visitor Georg Wallin (35) in 1710: '...on Sundays you don't travel by carriage or boat, because everything is then so quiet, that if London on other days is a noisy world, it is then like a holy Jerusalem. The same is true for all of England, yes it is impossible to get something to eat outside your house, because all the eating houses and taverns are closed, and if good friends hadn't invited me home, I would have had to make every Sunday a day of fasting. You cannot hear any singing, music or playing, because such things are, regardless of the occasion, prohibited and any violation will be heavily punished.'

Out of town diarists made a dutiful tour of the tourist sights of London, often shown round by the friends and relations they were staying with, or using guide books. Unlike some, Wallin (35) sensibly decided not to regurgitate the guide book in his diary: 'Since I have found everything thoroughly described in the *New View of London* it seems more a burden than a necessity to go through every detail'. Other aspects of the tourist experience are detailed by diarists. Joseph Hékékyan Bey (244) had trouble finding a hotel room in 1862: 'The Grosvenor was full, and after going the round of several hotels which were all full on account of their intrinsic worth in comfort and moderate charges we found the Queen's Hotel in Cork Street in which we found plenty of room, I suppose from the comparative low scale of its material resources and exorbitant charges. While I reposed I sent my wife and son to be driven in a hired carriage in the parks and the principal streets'. As well as seeing the Tower, St Paul's, Westminster Abbey and the Houses of Parliament and the museums, those who were in town in the autumn were usually taken to the Lord Mayor's Show, like Betty Fothergill (77) in 1769 and Elizabeth Huxtable (199) in 1818, and to any big public celebrations that coincided with their stay.

National events of all kinds elicited diary comments and description. John Wilkes (80) was in London during the Gordon riots in 1780: 'Attended the examination at Guildhall. In the Chamberlain's Office Charles Bird apprentice to John Lomas, Tallow-Chandler in Widgcombe Street, now in Clerkenwell Bridewell accused of setting fire to Lord Mansfield's House by Samuel Masters apprentice to Anthony Hook, Carver & Gilder, in Widgcombe Street. The father of Samuel Masters is Wm Masters at the King of Prussia's Head in John Street, Golden Square'. Robert Lee (388) watched a demonstration in favour of the Reform Bill in 1867: ' About three or half-past in the afternoon I left home with X [sic] to walk down to Eaton Place. We went through the Albany and found both sides of Piccadilly crowded with people. There were carts, omnibuses & carriages moving slowly along the road but no people in the road. I proposed to go into Pall Mall & across the Green Park to avoid the Crowd. On reaching P. Mall the procession had commenced and it was impossible to cross it. The men were not badly dressed. They walked I think 6 abreast and at a rapid pace. At intervals a band or banner passed. Occasionally there was a suppressed shout. We turned up St James Street and saw the club windows filled with the members looking out...' Monoroma Bose (**501**), an Indian student, recorded her horror at a terrorist attack in 1884: '...A few days ago a part of Victoria Station was blown up by dynamite, & since then another plot has been discovered to blow up Charing Cross & Paddington in the same way – what wicked diabolical men they must be who form such plots'. Nine years later Andrew Tait (**539**) was similarly agog: 'What d'you think has happened? The post office at New Cross, into which I have been scores of times, has been blown up by ANARCHISTS! Yes, all the front blown out and the place set on fire. Luckily no one was passing and the shop was shut for the night. The fire was put out and the letters saved with the exception of 4. The bomb was only in a cardboard case but for its size exceedingly destructive. Excitement reigns throughout New Cross...'

Local calamities were of particular appeal to diarists. In 1739 Stephen Monteage (**46**) wrote: 'This night about 10 a fire broke out at a Sugar Bakers near Colledge Hill which burnt verry furiously several hours, I pray God comfort the Afflicted and preserve us from the like Calamity. I hear it began at the Sugar House of Messrs Kidd and Harbin in Brickhill Lane, Thames Street...'. Elizabeth Elphinstone's children had a lucky escape on a day out from Enfield in 1801 (**128**): 'A singular and Awful circumstance marked this day. Elizth Willm & Jno went to see Waltham & soon after they left it in about 20 minutes the Powder Mills there Blew up with a tremendous Report which shook the Earth here – the belief it had happened on the very spot they had visited – the strange chance that had made them be there that day & the supposition of their narrow & Providential escape impressed my thoughts the whole Night'.

Subject-matter in the diaries revolves around domestic, social and working routines. These could vary considerably between individuals, but apart from that differs little between male and female diarists. It is sometimes assumed that more women than men kept diaries. The evidence of this checklist indicates otherwise, with the proportion of men to women diarists at 6:4. But children wrote diaries, too. In 1789 W Hugh Burgess (**108**), a St Marylebone schoolboy, recorded a family outing: 'We five dined at Captain Pouncies. After went in his coach to Deptford on board a Ship. I was sick riding in the Coach. Drank tea on board home at 9 o'clock, wet through'. There is the sad case of Raleigh Trevelyan (**176**) in 1813 – unhappy at school in Brentford, and then increasingly ill until his death the next year. Seven-year-old Quaker Anne Capper (**225**) began her beautifully written copperplate diary in 1824, with entries such as: 'At Tottenham Meeting this morning, we attended the marriage of Henry Cox and Harriet Cumine. I wore my pattens', and F S Girdlestone (**552**), a fifteen-year-old chorister at St Paul's in the year of Queen Victoria's Jubilee voiced a complaint still familiar on public occasions: 'Everything is now 'Jubilee'. Men in the street sell the ordinary penny toys as Jubilee toys'. From the later twentieth century come three Ealing schoolchildren who wrote about their life on Census Day in 1971. Diane Wong (**883**) and her family visited the West End. 'We went to Oxford Street and parked in one of the side streets. My father and two brothers walked down to Bayswater Road and looked at the paintings on display. My mother and I looked at the shop windows in Oxford Street. Most of the fashion was hot-pants and suede boots and shoes... afterwards we walked down Oxford Street to the Lyons Food Hall. Inside there are 6 different restaurants...'.

Children's diaries comprise a mere 3 per cent of the total here, but we also find glimpses of children through adult eyes in the diaries. In 1672 the Earl of Anglesey (**13**) mourned the death of his young granddaughter from smallpox: '... I went to Lincolne's Inn to church about 9 of the clock after I was gone she sweetly slept in the Lord... The 28th of this month she would have been 17 months old being borne Jan 28 about 5 in the evening... The child was buryed at 10 of the clock at night in St Martins chancell... Wrote to my son and comforted my daughter'. And in 1874 Robert Cust's son Robbie was causing him great concern. The boy was unhappy at Eton, where he felt bullied, and furthermore he was nervous of learning to ride, unlike his sisters. 'I took the Children to the Riding School. Here another malefication assailed me; the Girls galloped round and round beautifully – but Robbie refused to go out of walking pace – flung himself or was flung from the horse, and then made a frightful scene... However, <u>learn to ride he must</u>' (**440**). Childbirth also features in diaries. In 1885 Lady Avebury (**503**) blamed the death of General Gordon for the unexpectedly early arrival of her baby in 1885 : 'Baby born at 4.30 am. I began to feel ill about 10 o'clock. I had gone to bed at 9 & fast asleep when Gerty came in & told me Gordon was killed. I suppose it excited me. Luckily my nurse was in the house'.

The social origins of the majority of diarists in the checklist are predictably upper and middle class, though there are some working class examples. It is impossible to estimate the scale of working class diary-keeping. Fewer of these diaries survive, but that may be the result of home circumstances rather than a paucity of diarists. Upper and middle class families were perhaps more likely to have attics or other permanent storage space to which such family souvenirs could safely be relegated. Reading those working-class diaries that are still available gives one no sense that the writer thought him or herself in any way unusual to be keeping a diary. Among the examples here are George Jupp (**361**), an agricultural labourer on his way to New Zealand, Eli Rose (**545**), a builder's labourer working on mansion flats in Bloomsbury, and two servants – Thomas, a footman (**292**) and James Palmer (**433**), a coachman. The rest are mainly to be found among the diarists of the Second World War period.

As might be anticipated, the professional classes are well-represented among the diarists. Of the twenty-seven doctors' diaries listed, ranging from James Petiver in 1688 (**19**) to a medical student writing for Mass-Observation in 1943 (**846**), some of the most interesting are those of Thomas Silvester, founder of Clapham General Dispensary (**320**) and Henry Carter, of St George's Hospital (**338**). William Cooper (**145**) also provides a useful mixture of work and leisure: 'Heard an excellent sermon by Mr Winter in the morning and went in the afternoon to see Mr Nixon's leg'.

Churchgoing is commented on with great regularity in the diaries – 'A fine morning after a frost. Went to the Lock Chapel in the morning. Heard an excellent sermon by Dr Thorpe' wrote Charles De Coetlogon (**189**), in 1828, noting that he gave a shilling for the collection. The clergy themselves provide over forty of the items listed here. Dan Greatorex (**365**) was an energetic cleric employed by the Thames Church Mission in the 1850s, travelling about on their ship the *Swan*, visiting seamen. His very full diary details other activities too, as varied as attending services at the Lock Chapel, dining at Simpson's in the Strand, and seeing over the cable-laying ship, the *Agamemnon*. Canon Hall (**491**), of St Paul's, mixed in grander circles in 1892: 'Preached at S Paul's Cathedral. Administered Holy Communion to the Duke of Cambridge and the Grand Duchess of Mecklenburg-Strelitz'. Next day he 'lunched with Archdeacon Sinclair, & met the Duchess of Buckingham. I sat next to her & found her grace a very charming person, quick & clever & frank & without a trace of affectation. She is a fine woman of about thirty with good features & must have been very pretty when young.' Reginald Taylor (**826**), Vicar of St James, Islington, during the Second World War, had other concerns: 'Up late owing to raids at night. Chiefly on Swansea. Our grief at the decision of Parliament to open theatres and cinemas on Sunday because of its dishonour to God. Shopped and telephoned. Talk with gas men about worship'.

Over twenty diaries in this checklist were kept by lawyers, from Goddard Guyborn at Lincoln's Inn in 1642 (**4**) to F N E Starkey, working at a City law firm while waiting for his call-up in 1945 (**865**). And some diaries survive as a result of court cases. A notable example is that of Thomas Bridge (**62**), of Bread Street, a drug importer whose long series of diaries, covering 1760–1810, ended up as Chancery Masters' Exhibits at the Public Record Office. The lawyers' interest in the case is forgotten now, but the diaries themselves chronicle a long career in the import business, which Bridge combined with a country lifestyle in Tottenham, often commuting daily to the City.

The range of goods available in the London shops impressed most diarists, and shopping is a frequently recurring theme. Even Louis de Geer (**42**), who liked to sneer at all things English, admitted that London shops were worth a look during his 1728 visit: 'Quoiqu'il y ait toutes sortes de boutiques par milliers à Londres dans lesquelles on trouve toutes les marchandises imaginables, quoique à très haut prix, cependant il y en a une, qu'on nomme the great Toyshop, la grande boutique de nippes, qui mérite d'être vue.. il y a des richesses immenses...'. Men were every bit as enthusiastic as women in their pursuit of consumer goods. Thomas Wolley (**223**), about to go abroad in 1823, was keen to smarten up his wardrobe and get ready to pack: 'In London I went to Henry Franklyns where we breakfasted then went to the taylors to get a coat & pantaloons...Tried my new pantaloons on uncomfortable things pantaloons walked about London with my Father got a new spring to my powder flash at 4 went in a coach to Twickenham...went into the City got some tools. Dined at a coffee house coming home in the Coach met a German who advised me to get Richard's Guide de Voyage & Adlung's German grammar...We walked about London & I ordered a seal skin waistcoat'. Leonard Wyon (**373**) enjoyed impulse buying, bringing home little presents for his temperamental wife, May: 'Brought home a china candlestick & a melon for dear May' he records in August 1853. In 1932 Rosamonde Muspratt (**648**) was making regular forays to the London shops: 'Dash up to London to Gorringes sale and buy pyjamas and corduroys for John', 'Match china and look at Hamptons old furniture', 'Long day in town. Great hunt for red velvet dress...' are typical entries.

Almost all diarists, of any period, revert to enduring preoccupations such as health, food, and (this being England), the weather. Health is a particularly common topic. Diarists relate their current ailments and treatment : 'Had a most acute attack from spasm & obstruction of water which all blood, sent for Dr Ashburne & Mr Copeland who relieved me by his catheter twice that day, & three on Friday after being in the hot bath – calomel & senna operated well on Friday evg. The pain did not return & my water was of its proper colour. I attribute this attack to drinking half a wine glass of Port wine and a lump of sugar in a teaspoon of coffee after dinner on the 9th' wrote Samuel Boddington (**184**) in 1842. Other writers are moved to comment on their health on special days, such as New Year, or a birthday. Samuel Kevan's thirty-ninth birthday in 1803 (**136**) produced the mournful reflection: 'Saturday was my birthday making me 39 years I feel my decay more this year than I ever did – these Rheum^c Pains brings me down – tho blessed be the Lord I am much eased'. On New Year's Day in the same year William Upcott (**149**) was writing 'I never remember beginning a year with more unfavourable symptoms than the present. When I awoke at 8 o/c my body was in pain and my mind full of spleen and peevishness – owing to the Tooth Ache – which has grievously tormented this poor tenement of mine for the last two days'.

Meals at home and elsewhere were of great importance to many writers. The historian Edward Gibbon (**65**) dined out frequently, and was a regular at his club in 1762: 'That respectable body of which I have the honor to be a Member affords every evening a sight truly English. Twenty or thirty perhaps of the first men in the kingdom in point of fashion and fortune supping at little tables covered with a napkin, in the middle of a Coffee room, upon a bit of cold meat or a Sandwich & drinking a glass of Punch'. None of the diarists examined for this checklist had quite the same preoccupation with menus for which Parson Woodforde is so famous, though the actor John Pritt Harley (**397**) provides some competition. His consumption of food and drink in the last year of his life, 1854, leaves the reader wondering how he was able to go on stage, and may well have contributed to his fatal stroke: 'Dinner at four, roast mutton, potato, boiled plum pudding, brandy, biscuit, cheese, ale, port and sherry. Tea at six, theatre half past six, incl. Ellen, acted in one piece, home half past ten. Supped at eleven, cold roast mutton, biscuit, cheese, ale. Brandy and water and cake with Betsy. Bed at one'.

Entertainments of all kinds are described with relish. Picnic parties, excursions, visits to pleasure gardens – like Lady Mackintosh (**145**) in 1801 – 'after tea took Letitia to Vauxhall where I did not stay long enough to see the Duchess of Devonshire my inducement for going, & came home cold & comfortless between 11 & 12' – or the ubiquitous habits of opera- and theatregoing feature prominently. Maria Cust (**382**), just back from her honeymoon in 1856 'Went to the Lyceum Theatre to see Madame Ristori act 'Maria Stuarda' in the piece of that name. She is a wonderful tragic actress, but I hardly like her as well as Mlle Rachel'. Eliza Salvin (**337**) gained a different experience of the proceedings when invited to a dress rehearsal in 1859: 'Dress rehearsal of Henry V at the Princesses. A very curious sight. The theatre is lighted, but not so fully as during a representation. Kean sat in the centre of the dress circle. The actors hurried through their parts for it was not so much a rehearsal for the acting as for the scenery – Actors appear in the boxes every now & then to get a view of what they will never see again'. As a music student in 1901, Ethel Clementi (**559**) was a discriminating listener: 'As the Albert Hall was so crowded last Sunday & so many people had to be turned away, the entire programme was repeated to-day

& Olive & I got in in the 1s 6d's area stalls. The R A band performed & two lady singers who were decidedly poor. The programme included Chopin's funeral march & the Dead March in Saul'. The solemn programme was prompted by the recent death of Queen Victoria. Less cultural amusements were also popular. An anonymous Irish clergyman (**64**) joined friends for a summer walk in 1772: '...yesterday evening being very fine Tempted the Dr of the World, another gentleman & me to walk through the Fields to the Farthing Pye-house famous for cakes & Ale & the Amusement of some small Gentry who frequent it to play Ninepins & Skittles. We found at least 50 people Happily Employed on this occasion. Each of them as Happy as a King & many of them as Despotic & Arbitrary, having Long Pipes in their mouths & always smoaking their own Tobacco How offensive soever it may be to the Olfactory Nerves of their Neighbours.' In 1827 his compatriot the Irish journalist Edward Moran (**237**) 'Went for the first time to Tattersalls near Hyde Park Corner where the racing stud of the late Duke of York with his carriages dogs harness &c were disposed of by auction – an immense crowd – all the sporting people there...'. And Sir Charles Pasley (**305**) visited a freak show in 1846: 'See the two exhibitions in Regent Street the 3-legged Portuguese child 7 months old and cheerful & active with 2 legs... Also, fruit, fish and diseases, models of...'.

Crime, inevitably, affected some diarists personally. In 1778 Thomas Bridge (**62**) was the victim of a burglary at his home in Tottenham: 'I rose at 6. Was called by the Servants who had come down & found the House had been broke open viz they the Rogues had try'd to Wrench up the Windows of the china closet & Kitchen, Scullery & Pantry but could not. They then took up the paving before the Cellar window & worked a Hole under the Kerb & got into the Cellar then searched every Drawer & Closet in the Kitchen opend the China Closet & examined every part, broke open a small spice chest, all the knife cases, took carving knives by way of wepons which when they went they left on the floor in the Passage. They broke open two Beaufets & Ransacked the Drawers & drank...Brandy...' A very long list of stolen items follows. Emma Groom (**379**) reported a mugging in 1869: 'My Dear Brother William was Pushed Down by a Bad Woman who tried to get is Umbrella but did not succeed he fell with his Foot under him which caused Dislocation of Ancle and Fracture was taken to Bartholomew Hospital where he will remain for Some Time on Sunday May 30th I went to see him he was in very good spirits and Bears it Better than we Expected'. Eighteenth- and early nineteenth-century diarists sometimes recorded the aftermath of crime in the shape of public executions. 'Witnessed the execution of 5 men before Newgate' wrote Joseph Hunter (**129**) briskly in 1828.

Diarists enjoyed recording gossip and rumour and anecdotes of all kinds. Lord Broughton (**169**) mentions in 1818 that 'Mr Julius the apothecary of Richmond breakfasted with us – he told me that some one had proposed to Lord Sidmouth to send letter thro' tunnels by steam in 35 minutes to Bristol – Lord S told Julius this'. Adelaide Seymour (**319**) was enjoyably shocked in 1845: 'Heard this morning that the Companion of poor Adela Villiers's flight was a Captain Ibbetson of Lord Cardigan's Regiment to whom it appears she was married at Gretna Green on Thursday. Fancy poor Lady Jersey's horror at having a daughter called Lady Adela Ibbetson!' By 1914, an anonymous Kensington lady (**589**) was assiduously recording the daily rumours that came her way at the outbreak of the First World War, some very implausible, as in

10

'Heard that a German tried to erect a wireless station on top of the Ritz Hotel. He was arrested.', others less so: 'Heard that their neighbours at Caterham are avoiding speaking to Mrs Schilling, an Englishwoman whose husband became a naturalised Englishman several years ago, & is a manager in the Dresdener Bank. They started rumours that he had been arrested as a spy. The Dresdener Bank has been licenced by the Government to carry on business under supervision & conditions. If it has to close, the Schillings will be ruined'.

Books and current reading form a popular topic for diarists. Some maintain a list of what they have read, or intend to read, as part of the diary itself, but more usually the information is slotted into general passages. 'Worked at my table cover and read Milman's *History of Christianity*' wrote Lady Charlotte Lindsay in 1840 (**180**), but over the Christmas holidays she moved to lighter fare: 'finished all the published numbers of *Master Humphrey's Clock* in which there are some very pathetic touching scenes & some humorous characters'.

An incidental pleasure of some diaries is sketches or cartoons supplied by the writer, such as the charming family portraits in the margins of Andrew and Agnes Donaldson's diaries (**456**) and the illustrations of wartime life in those of W E Hall (**856**) and Percy Home (**858**). Home also included some cuttings and ephemera, including a bar bill for two cocktails. The diaries of Robert Ramsay (**495**), a long series, are stuffed with items he amassed in his daily activities: admission tickets, programmes, orders of service and much more. Ramsay's collection appears to have been random; other diarists deliberately mounted paper items in their diary by way of illustration. Perhaps the most attractive example listed here is that of the Newcastle businessman W J Bell (**354**) who created a neat scrapbook diary of his visit to London for the Great Exhibition. As well as writing a detailed account of all his doings, he stuck into the book a series of illustrations, maps, tickets and bills, providing an intriguing montage of London life in 1851.

Among the questions that this project has frequently prompted are: 'Nobody has time to write a diary these days, do they?', and, 'How do you know the diarists were telling the truth?' In response to the first question, the editor's reply is that you might be surprised. She has learned of a considerable number of diaries currently being written, though no one will openly declare their ultimate plans for the manuscripts. We must hope they will eventually be placed in suitable custody. There is also a thriving genre of internet diary-keeping under way, though most of it makes tedious reading. In reply to the second question, diaries should be treated with the same caution as any other historical evidence, with due allowance made for bias, special pleading and self-delusion. Most were not written for public consumption, at least not in the writer's lifetime. Those that were – notably those deliberately kept for publication, by journalists and politicians hoping to fulfil the maxim 'Keep a diary and one day it will keep you' – trail their own warnings about the author's intended effect and self-presentation.

Using the checklist

The checklist is arranged in order of each diary's starting date. In the case of a long-running diary containing a London section, the starting date given will be that of the London coverage, even if the diary began many years earlier. The entry then gives the diarist's name, titles, description and occupation, if known. Anonymous writers precede named ones within the chronological sequence. If the gender is not obvious, it has been added if identified. Details of the manuscript follow, with the abbreviated repository name and reference number. Some manuscript diaries are available on commercial microfilms, and this has been noted where found. There is a list of locations with addresses, an index of diarists and a subject index of coverage. The latter is of necessity fairly basic. It picks up subject terms used in checklist entry descriptions where that information was available, but the user should bear in mind that information about, say, 'coffee houses', 'Crystal Palace' or 'bomb damage' might well also occur in other diaries of the appropriate period although not specifically mentioned in their own entries and therefore not indexed to the term. Wives and children of clergy, medical practitioners, lawyers and the like have been indexed under those professions, to keep complementary material together.

Acknowledgements

The editor's thanks are due to all the archivists, librarians, museum staff and others, world-wide, who have given so much information, help and encouragement in producing this list. All are enthusiastic about encouraging greater use of their diary material, and will be delighted if this publication leads to its wider consultation. Thanks are also due to Mr Bengt Nilsson of Linköping University Library for translations from the Swedish.

LOCATIONS: ABBREVIATIONS AND ADDRESSES OF REPOSITORIES

American Phil S	American Philosophical Society, 104 South Fifth Street, Philadelphia, PA 19106–3387 USA
Australian NL	National Library of Australia, Canberra ACT, Australia 2600
Australian NMM	Australian National Maritime Museum, GPO Box 5131, Sydney NSW Australia 1042
Australian WM	Australian War Memorial, GPO Box 345, Canberra ACT, Australia 2601
Balliol	Balliol College Library, Oxford OX1 3BJ
Bank of England	Bank of England Archives, Threadneedle Street, London EC2R 8AH
Barclays	Barclays Bank Group Archives, Dallimore Road, Wythenshawe M23 9JA
Barings	ING Barings Holdings Ltd, 60 London Wall, London EC2M 5TQ
Barnet ALS	LB Barnet Archives & Local Studies Centre, c/o Hendon Library, The Burroughs, London NW4 4BQ
Bath CL	Bath Central Library, 19 The Podium, Northgate Street, Bath BA1 5AN
BBC WA	BBC Written Archives Centre, Peppard Road, Caversham Park, Reading, Berks. RG4 8TZ
Beds RO	Bedfordshire Record Office, County Hall, Caudwell Street, Bedford MK 42 9AP
Berks RO	Berkshire Record Office, Shinfield Park, Reading, Berks. RG2 9XD
Bexley LSAC	LB Bexley Local Studies Centre, Central Library, Townley Road, Bexleyheath DA6 7HJ
Billy Graham Center	Billy Graham Center, Wheaton College, 500 College Avenue, Wheaton, Ill. 60187–5593 USA
Birmingham CA	Birmingham City Archives, Central Library, Chamberlain Square, Birmingham B3 3HQ
Birmingham UL	Birmingham University Library, Edgbaston, Birmingham B15 2TT
Bishopsgate I	Bishopsgate Institute Library, 230 Bishopsgate, London EC2M 4QH
BL	British Library, 96 Euston Road, London NW1 2DB

13

BLOIO	British Library, Oriental and India Office Collection, 96 Euston Road, London NW1 2DB
Bodleian MS	Bodleian Library Manuscripts Department, Broad Street, Oxford OX1 3BG
Border Regt Mus	Border Regiment Museum, Queen Mary's Tower, The Castle, Carlisle CA3 8UR
Brasenose	Brasenose College Library, Oxford OX1 4AJ
Bristol U Theatre Colln	Bristol University Theatre Collection, Dept of Drama, Cantocks Close, Woodland Road, Bristol BS8 1UP
Bromley AS	LB Bromley Archive Service, Central Library, High Street, Bromley, Kent BR1 1EX
Bucks RO	Buckinghamshire Record Office, County Hall, Aylesbury, Bucks. HP20 1UU
Cambridge CRO	Cambridge Record Office, Shire Hall, Castle Hill, Cambridge CB3 0AP
Camden LSAC	LB Camden Local Studies and Archives Centre, Holborn Library, 32–38 Theobalds Road, London WC1X 8PA
Canterbury UL	Macmillan Brown Library, University of Canterbury, Private Bag 4800, Christchurch, New Zealand
Cape Town UL	Cape Town University Libraries, Private Bag 7701, Rondesbosch, South Africa
Cardiff CL	Cardiff Central Library, St David's Link, Frederick Street, Cardiff CF10 2DU
Carlisle PL	Carlisle Public Library, 11 Globe Lane, Carlisle CA3 8NX
Centre for Kentish Studies	Centre for Kentish Studies, County Hall, Maidstone, Kent ME14 1XQ
Cheshire CALSS	Cheshire and Chester Archives and Local Studies Service, Duke Street, Chester CH1 1RL
Chetham	Chetham's Library, Long Millgate, Manchester M3 1SB
Cornwall RO	Cornwall County Record Office, County Hall, Truro TR1 3AY
Courtauld	Courtauld Institute of Art, University of London, Somerset House, Strand, London WC2R 0RN
Croydon LSL	LB Croydon Local Studies Library, Croydon Clocktower, Katharine Street, Croydon, Surrey CR9 1ET
CUL	Cambridge University Library, West Road, Cambridge CB3 9DR
Cumbria RO	Cumbria Record Office, The Castle, Carlisle CA3 8UR
Denbighs RO	Denbighshire Record Office, The Old Rectory, Hawarden CH5 3NR
Derbys RO	Derbyshire Record Office, County Offices, Matlock DE4 3AG
Devon RO	Devon Record Office, Castle Street, Exeter, EX4 3PU
Doncaster A	Doncaster Archives, King Edward Road, Balby, Doncaster DN4 0NA

Dorset RO	Dorset Record Office, Bridport Road, Dorchester DT1 1RP
Duke UL	Duke University, William Perkins Library, Durham NC 27708 USA
Dulwich Coll	Dulwich College, Wodehouse Library, College Road, Dulwich, London SE21 7LD
Durham CRO	Durham County Record Office, County Hall, Durham DH1 5UL
E Kent AC	East Kent Archives Centre, Enterprise Business Park, Honeywood Road,Whitfield, Dover CT16 3EH
E R Yorks A	East Riding of Yorkshire Archives, County Hall, Beverley HU17 9BA
E Sussex RO	East Sussex Record Office, The Maltings, Castle Precincts, Lewes BN7 1YT
Ealing LHL	LB Ealing Local History Library, Central Library, 103 Ealing Broadway Centre, London W5 5JY
Enfield LHU	LB Enfield Local History Unit, Southgate Town Hall, Green Lanes, London N13 4XD
Essex RO	Essex Record Office, Wharf Road, Chelmsford CM2 6YT
Essex UL	University of Essex Library, Wivenhoe Park, Colchester CO4 3SQ
Fawcett L	Fawcett Library, London Guildhall University, Calcutta House, Old Castle Street, London E1 7NT
Filson HS	Filson Historical Society, 1310 South Third Street, Louisville, KY 40208 USA
Flints RO	Flintshire Record Office, The Old Rectory, Hawarden CH5 3NR
Friends' House	Religious Society of Friends Library, 173–77 Euston Road, London NW1 2BJ
Glos RO	Gloucestershire Record Office, Clarence Row, off Alvin Street, Gloucester GL1 3DW
Greenwich LHL	LB Greenwich Local History Library, Woodlands, Mycenae Road, London SE23 7SE
Guildhall L	Guildhall Library Manuscripts Section, Aldermanbury, London EC2P 2EJ
Hackney AD	LB Hackney Archives Department, 43 De Beauvoir Road, London N1 5SQ
Hammersmith ALHC	LB Hammersmith & Fulham Archives and Local History Centre, The Lilla Huset, 191 Talgarth Road, London W6 8BJ
Hants RO	Hampshire Record Office, Sussex Street, Winchester SO23 8TH
Haringey BC	LB Haringey Archives Service, Bruce Castle Museum, Lordship Lane, London N17 8NU
Harrow LHC	LB Harrow Local History Centre, Civic Centre Library, Box 4, Station Road, Harrow HA1 2UU
Harvard UL	Harvard University, Houghton Library, Cambridge, MA 02138 USA

Haverford Coll	Magill Library, Haverford College, 370 Lancaster Avenue, Haverford, PA 19041–1392 USA
Hereford RO	Hereford Record Office, The Old Barracks, Harold Street, Hereford HR1 2QX
Herts ALS	Hertfordshire Archives and Local Studies, County Hall, Hertford SG13 8EJ
Highgate LSI	Highgate Literary and Scientific Institution, 11 South Grove, London N6 6BS
Hornsey HS	Hornsey Historical Society, The Old Schoolhouse, 136 Tottenham Lane, London N8 7EL
Hounslow LSL	LB Hounslow Local Studies Library, 24 Treaty Centre, High Street, Hounslow, Middx. TW3 1ES
Huguenot L	Huguenot Library, University College, Gower Street, London WC1E 6BT
Hull UL	Hull University Library, Cottingham Road, Hull, HU6 7RX
Huntingdon CRO	Huntingdon County Record Office, Grammar School Walk, Huntingdon PE29 3LF
Huntington L	Huntington Library, 1151 Oxford Road, San Marino, CA 91108 626–405 USA
I Classical S	Institute of Classical Studies, University of London, Senate House, Malet Street, London WC1E 7HU
I Education	Institute of Education Library, University of London, 20 Bedford Way, London WC1H 0AL
IEE	Institution of Electrical Engineers, Archives Dept., Savoy Place, London WC2R 0BL
Illinois UL	Illinois University Library, 1408 W. Gregory Drive, Urbana, IL 61801 USA
IOW CRO	Isle of Wight County Record Office, 26 Hillside, Newport PO30 2EB
Islington LHC	LB Islington Local History Collection, Central Reference Library, 2 Fieldway Crescent, London N5 1PF
IWM	Imperial War Museum, Department of Documents, Lambeth Road, London SE1 6HZ
John Rylands L	John Rylands Library, University of Manchester, 150 Deansgate, Manchester M3 3EH
KB	Stockholm Royal Library, Box 5039, S–102 41 Stockholm, Sweden
Kensington LSL	LB Kensington Local Studies Library, Hornton Street, London W8 7RX
Kings Coll	Cambridge Modern Archives Centre, King's College, Cambridge CB2 1ST
Kingston MHS	LB Kingston-upon-Thames Museum and Heritage Service, North Kingston Centre, Richmond Road, Kingston-upon-Thames KT2 5PE
L Congress	Library of Congress, 101 Independence Avenue SE, Washington DC 20540 USA

Lambeth AD   LB Lambeth Archives Department, Minet Library, 52 Knatchbull Road, London SE5 9QY

Lambeth Palace L   Lambeth Palace Library, London SE1 7JU

Lancs RO   Lancashire Record Office, Bow Lane, Preston PR1 8ND

Leeds CL   Leeds Central Library, Calverley Street, Leeds LS1 3AB

Leeds UL   University of Leeds, Brotherton Library, Leeds LS2 9JT

Leics RO   Record Office for Leicestershire, Leicester and Rutland, Long Street, Wigston Magna, Leicester LE18 2AH

Lewis Walpole L   Lewis Walpole Library, Farmington, CT 06032 USA

Lewisham LSC   LB Lewisham Local Studies Centre, 199–201 Lewisham High Street, London SE13 6LG

Lincs Archives   Lincolnshire Archives, St Rumbold Street, Lincoln LN2 5AB

Linköping DCL   Linköping Diocesan and County Library, Box 1984, 581 19 Linköping, Sweden

Linley Sambourne H   Linley Sambourne House, 18 Stafford Terrace, London W8 7BH

Linnean S   Linnean Society Library, Burlington House, Piccadilly, London W1V 0LQ

LISWA   Library & Information Service of Western Australia, JS Battye Library of Western Australian History, Alexander Library Building, Perth Cultural Centre, Perth, WA Australia 6000

Liverpool RO   Liverpool Record Office and Local History Library, William Brown Street, Liverpool L3 8EW

LMA   London Metropolitan Archives, 40 Northampton Road, London EC1R 0HB

London L   London Library, 14 St James Square, London SW1Y 4LG

LSE   British Library of Political and Economic Science, London School of Economics, Houghton Street, Aldwych, London WC2A 2AE

Lund UB   Lund Universitetsbibliotek, PO Box 134, 221 00 Lund, Sweden

M New Zealand   Museum of New Zealand, PO Box 467, Wellington, New Zealand

Manchester ALS   Manchester Archives and Local Studies, Central Library, St Peter's Square, Manchester M2 5PD

Maryland HS   Maryland Historical Society, 201 West Monument Street, Baltimore, MD 21201–4674 USA

Massachusetts HS   Massachusetts Historical Society, 1154 Boylston Street, Boston, MA 02215–3695 USA

Mercers' Co Archives   Worshipful Company of Mercers, Mercers' Hall, Ironmonger Lane, London EC2V 8HE

Michigan UL	Michigan University Library, Ann Arbor, MI 48109 USA
Minnesota HS	Minnesota Historical Society, 345 W. Kellogg Blvd, St Paul, MN 55102–1906 USA
Missouri UL	Missouri University Library, 8001 Natural Bridge Road, St Louis, MO 63121 USA
M-O	Mass-Observation Archive, University of Sussex Library, Falmer, Brighton BN1 9QL
MoL	Museum of London, 150 London Wall, London EC2Y 5HN
N Carolina UL	North Carolina University Library, Southern Historical Collection, Wilson Library, Chapel Hill, NC 27599–3938 USA
N Yorks CRO	North Yorkshire County Record Office, County Hall, Northallerton DL7 8AF
NAL	National Art Library, Victoria and Albert Museum, Cromwell Road, London SW7 2RL
NAS	National Archives of Scotland, HM General Register House, Edinburgh EH1 3YY
Nat Army M	National Army Museum, Dept. of Archives, Royal Hospital Road, London SW3 4HT
Nat L Ireland	National Library of Ireland, Kildare Street, Dublin 2, Ireland
Nat L Scotland	National Library of Scotland, Dept. of MSS, George IV Bridge, Edinburgh EH1 1EW
Nat L Wales	National Library of Wales, Aberystwyth SY23 3BU
Nat Maritime M	National Maritime Museum, Manuscripts Section, Greenwich, London SE10 9NF
Nat Portrait G	National Portrait Gallery, Heinz Archive, St Martin's Place, London WC2H 0HE
Nat Railway M	National Railway Museum, Leeman Road, York YO26 4XJ
NE Lincs Archives	North East Lincolnshire Archives, Town Hall, Grimsby DN31 1HX
Nelson Provincial M	Nelson Provincial Museum, PO Box 853, Nelson 7015, New Zealand
New Hampshire HS	New Hampshire Historical Society, The Tuck Library, 30 Park Street, Concord NH 03301-6384 USA
New York HS	New York Historical Society, 170 Central Park West, New York, NY 10024 USA
New York PL	New York Public Library, 5th Avenue and 42nd Street, New York, NY 10018–2788 USA
Newham LSL	LB Newham Local Studies Library, Stratford Reference Library, Water Lane, London E15 4NJ
NLJ	National Library of Jamaica, 12 East Street, Kingston, Jamaica
Norfolk RO	Norfolk Record Office, Gildengate House, Anglia Square, Upper Green Lane, Norwich NR3 1AX

Norrköping CL	Norrköping City Library, Box 2113, 600 02 Norrköping, Sweden
Northants RO	Northamptonshire Record Office, Wootton Hall Park, Northampton NN4 8BQ
Northumberland AS	Northumberland Archives Service, Melton Park, North Gosforth, Newcastle upon Tyne NE3 5QX
Notts Archives	Nottinghamshire Archives, County House, Castle Meadow Road, Nottingham NG2 1AG
Oxfordshire Archives	Oxfordshire Archives, St Luke's Church, Temple Road, Cowley, Oxford OX4 2EX
Parliamentary A	Parliamentary Archives, House of Lords, London SW1A 0PW
Pennsylvania HS	Pennsylvania Historical Society, 1300 Locust Street, Philadelphia, PA 19107 USA
Philadelphia Arch HRC	Philadelphia Archdiocesan Historical Research Center, 100 East Wynnewood Road, Wynnewood, PA 19096–3001 USA
Plymouth and W Devon RO	Plymouth and West Devon Record Office, Unit 3, Clare Place, Coxside, Plymouth PL4 0JW
Private	In private hands. Address given if known.
PRO	Public Record Office, Ruskin Avenue, Kew, Richmond, Surrey TW9 4DU
PRONI	Public Record Office of Northern Ireland, 66 Balmoral Avenue, Belfast BT9 6NY
Punch L	*Punch* Library and Archives, Trevor House, 100 Brompton Road, London SW3 1ER
QMW	Queen Mary College Library, Mile End Road, London E1 4NS
R Academy	Royal Academy of Arts, Burlington House, Piccadilly, London W1V 0DS
R Coll Physicians	Royal College of Physicians of London, 11 St Andrew's Place, Regents Park, London NW1 4LE
R Opera House	Royal Opera House Archives, Covent Garden, London WC2E 9DD
Radcliffe I	Schlesinger Library, Radcliffe Institute for Advanced Study, Harvard University, 10 Garden Street, Cambridge, MA 02138–3630 USA
Reading UL	Reading University Library, PO Box 223, Whiteknights, Reading RG6 6AE
Regents PC	Regent's Park College, Angus Library, Pusey Street, Oxford OX1 2LB
Rhodes HL	Rhodes House Library, South Parks Road, Oxford OX1 3RG
Richmond LC	LB Richmond-upon-Thames Local Collections, Central Reference Library, Old Town Hall, Whittaker Avenue, Richmond TW9 1TP
Rutgers UL	Rutgers University Library, New Brunswick NJ 08903 USA

S Antiq	Society of Antiquaries of London, Burlington House, Piccadilly, London W1J 0BE
S Carolina UL	South Carolina University Library, Columbia, SC 29208 USA
S Tyneside CL	South Tyneside Central Library, Prince Georg Square, South Shields NE33 2PE
Shropshire RRC	Shropshire Records and Research Centre, Castle Gates, Shrewsbury SY1 2AQ
SOAS	School of Oriental and African Studies, University of London, Thornhaugh Street, London WC1H 0XG
Somerset ARS	Somerset Archive and Record Service, Obridge Road, Taunton TA2 7PU
Southampton UL	Southampton University Library, Special Collections, Highfield Road, Southampton SO17 1BJ
Southwark LSL	LB Southwark Local Studies Library, 211 Borough High Street, London SE1 1JA
St Deiniol's L	St Deiniol's Library, Hawarden CH5 3DF
St John's Coll Cambridge	St John's College Library, Cambridge CB2 1TP
St Paul's Cathedral L	St Paul's Cathedral Library, The Chapter House, St Paul's Churchyard, London EC4M 8AD
Staffs RO	Staffordshire Record Office, County Buildings, Eastgate Street, Stafford ST16 2LZ
State L NSW	State Library of New South Wales, Mitchell Library, Macquarie Street, Sydney, NSW Australia 2000
State L S Australia	State Library of South Australia, Mortlock Library, North Terrace, Adelaide, South Australia 5000
State L Victoria	State Library of Victoria, 328 Swanston Street, Melbourne, Victoria, Australia 3000
Suffolk RO (Bury)	Suffolk Record Office, Raingate Street, Bury St Edmunds IP33 2AR
Suffolk RO (Lowestoft)	Suffolk Record Office, Central Library,Clapham Road, Lowestoft NR32 1DR
Surrey HC	Surrey History Centre, 130 Goldsworth Road, Woking GU21 1ND
Sutton AS	LB Sutton Archives Section, Central Library, St Nicholas Way, Sutton SM1 1EA
Thurrock M	Thurrock Museum, Orsett Road, Grays, Thurrock RM17 5DX
Tower Hamlets LHLA	LB Tower Hamlets Local History Library and Archives, Bancroft Library, 277 Bancroft Road, London E1 4DQ
Tyne and Wear AS	Tyne and Wear Archives Service, Blandford House, Blandford Square, Newcastle-upon-Tyne NE1 4JA
U London L	University of London Library, Senate House, Malet Street, London WC1E 7HU
UC London	University College London Library, Gower Street, London WC1E 6BT

UCal Berkeley	University of California at Berkeley, Bancroft Library, Berkeley, CA 94720–6000 USA
UL Wales Bangor	University of Wales Library, Bangor, Dept. of MSS, Bangor, Gwynedd LL57 2DG
Virginia UL	Virginia University Library, Charlottesville, VA 22901 USA
W Yorks AS	West Yorkshire Archives Service, Chapeltown Road, Sheepscar, Leeds LS7 3AP
Wales UL	University of Wales Library, Hugh Owen Building, Aberystwyth SY23 3DY
Waltham Forest ALHL	LB Waltham Archives and Local History Library, Vestry House Museum, Vestry Road, London E17 9NH
Wandsworth LHS	LB Wandsworth Local History Service, Battersea Library, 265 Lavender Hill, London SW11 1JB
Warwick MRC	Modern Records Centre, Warwick University Library, Coventry CV4 7AL
Warwicks CRO	Warwickshire County Record Office, Priory Park, Cape Road, Warwick CV34 4JS
WCA	Westminster City Archives, 10 St Ann's Street, London SW1P 2DE
Wellcome	Wellcome History of Medicine Library, 183 Euston Road, London NW1 2BE
Wesley Coll Bristol	Wesley College, College Park Drive, Henbury Road, Bristol BS10 7QD
Wigan AS	Wigan Archives Service, Town Hall, Leigh WN7 2DY
Wilts RO	Wiltshire & Swindon Record Office, County Hall, Bythesea Road, Trowbridge BA14 8BS
Wimbledon M	Wimbledon Society Museum, 26 Lingfield Road, London SW19 4QD
Winterthur M	Winterthur Museum, Winterthur, DE 19735 USA
Worcs RO	Worcestershire Record Office, County Hall, Spetchley Road, Worcester WR5 2NP
Yale UL	Yale University Library, PO Box 208240, New Haven, CT 06520–8240 USA
York City Archives	York City Archives, Art Gallery Building, Exhibition Square, York YO1 2EW
Yorks Archaeol S	Yorkshire Archaeological Society, Claremont, 23 Clarendon Road, Leeds LS2 9NZ
Zeeuwse B	Zeeuwse Bibliotheek, Kousteensedijk 7, 4331 JE, Middelburg, Netherlands

CHECKLIST OF UNPUBLISHED DIARIES

1. *1581* STONELEY, Richard, a teller of the Exchequer. Diary extracts, 1581, 1593, 1596. Bodleian MS Douce d.44 pp.69–104.

2. *1628* SKIPWITH, *Sir* Fulmar, of Newbold Hall, Broome, Warwicks. Mf of fragmented diary extracts, 1628–67, which include much time spent in London. Warwicks CRO MI213

3. *1640* TOWNSHEND, Henry, of Elmley Lovett, Worcs. Civil War diary, including events in London and Worcester, 1640–3. Worcs RO 899:192, 705:291

4. *1642* GODDARD, Guyborn, of Lincoln's Inn, lawyer. Diary, 1642, dealing with everyday life including having his portrait painted, his health problems, leisure, shopping and legal matters. Records numbers of plague dead each month. An edition is in preparation by Hazel Forsyth of the Museum of London's staff. MoL 46.78/735

5. *1646* CULLUM, *Sir* Thomas, of Hardwick, Suffolk, sheriff of London. Diary, 1646–7, of his daily life, also covering his work as sheriff of London. Suffolk RO (Bury) E2/29/1.2

6. *1655* JAMES, William, of Westminster School, schoolmaster. Diary, Jan–May 1655, his life as teacher at Westminster School, ill-health, medical treatment. In Latin. Bodleian MS Rawlinson d.216

7. *1656* DERING, *Sir* Edward, *2nd Bart*, of Surrenden, Kent, and Bloomsbury, Member of Parliament. Diary (Ephemeris), 1656–62; diary, 1673–5, of country life and visits to London, with business and pleasure there, financial preoccupations. Huntington L Other Collns; Centre for Kentish Studies Uncat'd U2981

8. *1661* LILLIE, Axel, *Count,* Swedish traveller. Diary of visit to England, 1661, including London. In Swedish. Lund UB De la Gardie/Lillie/10

9. *1666* ANON, a companion of the Earl of Sandwich on mission to Spain. Diary, 1666, of diplomatic mission to Spain, but including an account of the Fire of London. Chetham's A.2.122

10. *1666* RICH, Mary, of Leighs Priory, Felsted, Essex, *Countess of Warwick*. Diary, 1666–77, including London visits to family and for shopping. Much examination of conscience, but also detail on daily life and events. BL Add MSS 27,351–5

11. *1672* WALKER, John, of Coker Court, Somerset. Diary of travels, including London, 1672. Somerset ARS DD/WHb 3087

12. *1675* ANON, of Wonston, Hants, schoolmaster. Diary, 1675–8, including unsuccessful search for work in London and visits there from Colchester where he found a post. Bodleian MS Rawlinson d.1114 f.1–77

13. *1675* ANNESLEY, Arthur, *1st Earl of Anglesey*, Lord Privy Seal. Diary, 1675–84, continuing the earlier volume covering 1671–5 printed in HMC 13th Report Appdx. VI (1893). Official business, family news, social life. BL Add MSS 18730

14. *1677* THORESBY, Ralph, of Leeds, topographer. Diary of travels, including London, 1677–1724. Extracts in *Diary of Ralph Thoresby FRS* (ed J Hunter, 1830). Yorks Archaeol S MS 21–5

15. *1680* HARLEY, Robert, of Kinsham, Herefs, lawyer, of the Inner Temple. Diary, May–June 1680, of journey to London and stay there; coffee houses, clubs, entertainment. Bodleian MS Eng. misc. f.52

16. *1681* ASTON, *Sir* Willoughby, of Aston Hall, Cheshire, sheriff of Cheshire. Diary, 1681–1702, covering country life and visits to London. Liverpool RO 920 MD 172–5

17. *1684* TAYLOR, John, volunteer soldier. Diary, 1684–9, 'Multum in Parvo, or, History of his Life and Travells in America and other parts...' which covers his service as a volunteer in a regiment raised to oppose Monmouth (including in London) and his subsequent voyage to the West Indies. NLJ MS 105

18. *1684* WHITLEY, Roger, Member of Parliament for Chester. Diary, 1684–97, with much London material. An edition for the Lancashire and Cheshire Record Society is in preparation. Bodleian MS Eng. Hist. c. 711

19. *1688* PETIVER, James, medical practitioner, apothecary to the Charterhouse, botanist. Diary, 1688–93, about his work at the Charterhouse and personal affairs. Also his medical journal, 1687–1710. Both in small format with many abbreviations. BL Sloane 4024, 3220–6

20. *1690* KIRK, Robert, Gaelic scholar. Diary of his time in London, 1690, supervising printing of Bedell's Gaelic Bible. Edinburgh UL Laing III.545 Edition in preparation by Mark Goldie and Claire Jackson.

21. *1690* PURSLOW, Norris, of Wapping, clothier. Diary, *c.*1690–1737. Each page has astrological drawing. His private and business life, with emphasis on illnesses and misfortunes, all related to their astrological significance. He was probably a Quaker. Wellcome MS 4021

22. *1697* BRYDGES, James, later *1st Duke of Chandos*, Member of Parliament for Hereford. Diary, 1697–1702, of daily activities, social and political. Huntington L Stowe Colln Brydges Papers

23. *1698* GYLDENSTOLPE, Carl Adolf, Swedish nobleman, army officer, brother of Edward Gyldenstolpe (**24**). Diary of visit to London, 1698, with his brother. Sights of London, contacts, impressions. Tower of London, St Paul's cathedral, Royal Exchange. In French. KB Stockholm M 244:1

1. Count Edward Gyldenstolpe (**24**) from Sweden visits Chelsea Hospital in 1698 *(courtesy of the Royal Library, Stockholm)*

24. *1698* GYLDENSTOLPE, Edward, Swedish nobleman, army officer, brother of Carl Adolf Gyldenstolpe (**23**). Diary of visit to London, 1698, with his brother. Sights of London, contacts, impressions. In English. KB Stockholm M 244:2

25. *1704* ISHAM, *Sir* Justinian, *4th Bart*, of Lampton Hall, Northants. Diary, 1704–36, including trips to London. Northants RO Isham 20

26. *1704* OSBORNE, Thomas, *1st Duke of Leeds*, statesman. Private diary, 1 Jan 1704–12 July 1712. Family travels, illnesses, deaths. BL Add MSS 28,041

27. *1705* WAKE, William, Archbishop of Canterbury. Diary, 7 March 1705–25 Jan 1725. He became Archbishop in 1716. Lambeth Palace L MS 1770

28. *1706* ANON, (female) of London. Diary, Sept 1706–March 1707, mentioning Newington, Islington and Bow churches. Bodleian MS Rawlinson d.1334

29. *1706* BRIGGINS, Peter, of Bartholomew Close, tobacco merchant. Diary, 1706–8, covering work, weather, Quaker meetings. Part of the Howard and Eliot family archives. LMA ACC 1017/2

30. *1707* ANON, (male) of London, wigmaker. Diary, Sept 1707–March 1709, religious and social affairs. Bodleian MS Rawlinson *c*.861

31. *1707* ANON, of Wanstead, Quaker. Portion of diary, 1707–15. Essex RO D/DK/F1

32. *1707* BELSON, Edward, of Reading, Berks. Diary, 1707–9, of life in London and Berkshire. Berks RO D/EX12/1

33. *1708* BENNET, Charles, of Dawley, Middx, *Baron Ossulston*, later *1st Earl of Tankerville*. Diary, 1708–12. Daily domestic and social engagements, frequent visits to London. Wife's ill-health and death in May 1710, concerns about his six children, expenses and accounts. Diary survives among Chancery Masters' exhibits for a court case. PRO C104/113 pt.2

34. *1709* PRINCE, Thomas, of Boston, Mass, clergyman. Diary, 1709–11, including trips to London. Massachusetts HS

35. *1710* WALLIN, Georg, Swedish student, traveller. Diary, 1708–10, of his travels round Europe. He was in London for a few months in the spring and summer of 1710. In Swedish. Linköping DCL G 14 a:2

36. *1711* ANON, (male) of London. Diary, Jan 1711–Aug 1712 with business details: collection of rents and debts, household purchases, food, churchgoing, coffeehouses. Bodleian MS Rawlinson d.1114

37. *1714* COWPER (née CLAVERING), Mary, *Countess*, Lady of the Bedchamber, 2nd wife of 1st Earl Cowper. Diary, 1714–23, with gaps, of court gossip and scandal. Available on Women's Language and Experience mf pt.1 (Adam Matthew, 1996). Herts ALS D/EP

38. *1717* SMITH, Carleton, Photocopy and transcript of his diary, April–July 1717 while in charge of state prisoners at Newgate after the 1715 Jacobite rebellion. Original destroyed in 1941. There is an index to text. Guildhall L MS 17,875/1–2; index at MS 17,876

39. *1722* DAWSON, John, of Hoxton Market, excise man and book collector. Diary, 1722–63. He left his extensive book collection, including the diaries, to Shoreditch parish; it is a rare survival of a parochial library. Hackney AD M3215

40. *1722* LUTTRELL, Narcissus, of Little Chelsea, Member of Parliament. Diary of 'private transactions' 1722–5, written in English but in Greek characters. BL Add MSS 10477

41. *1724* SOUTHWELL, Edward [?]. Diary of travel, including London, 1724. Extracts in *Country Life* (8 Feb 1973). Yorks Archaeol S MS 328

42. *1728* DE GEER, Louis. Swedish industrialist and government official. Diary of travels, including London in 1728. Tourist sights, social contacts. In French. He disliked most things English. Norrköping CL Finspong Colln

43. *1728* GRANO, John Baptist (Giovanni Battista), trumpeter. Prison diary, May 1728–Sept 1729, while in the Marshalsea for debt. Prison life, his benefit concerts. Bodleian MS Rawlinson d.34

44. *1732* BRYDGES, Henry, *2nd Duke of Chandos*, courtier. Diary, 1732–71, of court and social life. He succeeded to the dukedom in 1744. Huntington L Stowe Colln. Brydges Papers

45. *1732* HOWELL, Joshua, Rector of Lanreath, Cornwall, clergyman. Diary of visit to London, 1732. Cornwall RO HL(2)193

46. *1733* MONTEAGE, Stephen, of South Sea House and Custom House, accountant. Diary, 1733–64, chiefly on family, personal and business matters. Clear hand, good on social activities. Guildhall L MS 205/1–9

47. *1735* MORRIS, Robert Hunter, of New York City. Business diary, April 1735–Jan 1736, while travelling with his father. Much on social and business life in London. He made a later visit in 1749. Extracts in *Pennsylvania Magazine of History and Biography*, XIV (1940). L Congress Peter Force Papers 8D 108, also mf 17,137 reel 51

48. *1744* ANON, of Somerset. Diary of travel, including London, 1744. Possibly a companion of Thomas Carew (**49**). Somerset ARS DD/TB/14/25

49. *1744* CAREW, Thomas, of Crowcombe Court, Somerset. Diary of travel, including London, 1744. Somerset ARS DD/TB/18/4

50. *1747* GOUGH, Richard, of Enfield, antiquary. Diary, Aug 1747–Jan 1773 (gap 1751–5), mostly about Enfield. Bodleian MS Top.gen.e.6

51. *1748* BOSCAWEN, the Hon Frances Evelyn, of London and St Michael, Cornwall. Diary, Jan–Dec 1748, kept for her admiral husband. Daily life of family in London, amusements, reading. Bodleian MS Eng. Misc. f.71

52. *1748* NICOLSON, Thomas, of Perquimans County, NC, Quaker writer. Nicolson's diary runs from 1748–71, and includes a detailed account of his visit to England, including London, 26 Feb 1748–3 Oct 1750. N Carolina UL SB Weeks Papers (762)

53. *1750* LEE, William, of Totteridge Park, Herts. Diary, 1750–3. Herts ALS Acc 2967

54. *1751* BRYDGES, James, *3rd Duke of Chandos*, courtier, earlier a Member of Parliament. Diary, 1751–88 of political, court and social life. He succeeded to the dukedom in 1771. Huntington L Stowe Colln Brydges Papers

55. *1752* HAGEN, Jacob II, of London, merchant. Diary, 1752, 1780–90. Bodleian MS Eng. misc. f.77; *c.*250

56. *1753* HANBURY WILLIAMS, Frances [?], later *Countess of Essex*, daughter of Sir Charles Hanbury Williams. Diary, 1753, of a daughter (probably Frances) of Sir Charles Hanbury Williams, providing a 'complete picture of a fashionable young lady's social round' of London entertainments. Herts ALS M299

57. *1756* BRAY, William, of Shere, Surrey, and Great Russell Street, solicitor, county historian. Diary, 1756–1832 including frequent references to his London activities such as dinners, meetings of the Society of Antiquaries, research in the State Paper Office and Tower. Surrey HC G85/1/1–76

58. *1756* DICKINSON, Marshe, of London, Lord Mayor. Public diary, 1756–7 during his mayoralty, with some material on his private life. Guildhall L MS 100

59. *1757* ELIOT, John, merchant, underwriter. Diary, Feb–Nov 1757, with fairly detailed account of daily life, social engagements, meetings attended, visit to Cornwall. LMA ACC 1017/944

60. *1759* COURTNEY, John, of Beverley, Yorks. Diary, 1759–68, 1788–1805. He travelled widely and several times visited London, writing about the sights and his entertainment there. A published edition by Dr David Neave and Dr Susan Neave is in preparation. Hull UL DDX/60/1–4

61. *1759* HOLLIS, Thomas, of London, antiquary. Diary, 1759–70, of everyday life and activities, antiquarian work, learned societies, coffee houses, charities. Harvard UL MS Eng 1191

62. *1760* BRIDGE, Thomas, of Bread Street, and Tottenham, drug importer and merchant. Diary, 1760–1811, covering his work as a drug importer, business contacts, coffee house meetings etc, his family and social life, a burglary, and smallholding activities at his home in Tottenham. Mentions Gordon riots. PRO J90/13–14

63. *1760* PRICE, John, of Oxford, later Bodley's librarian. Summer travel diary, June 1760, Aug 1761, Sept 1761, 1763 including London visits. Bodleian MS Top.gen. f.33–4

64. *1761* ANON, of Ireland, clergyman. Full accounts of two visits to London from Dublin, Aug–Oct 1761 and Aug–Sept 1772, including both journeys. Lively, entertaining descriptions of sightseeing excursions, shopping, churches and other buildings, friends and acquaintances, written for the amusement of those at home. Extracts in *London Topographical Record*, XXVIII (2001). BL Add MSS 27951

65. *1761* GIBBON, Edward, historian. Diary, 4 Aug 1761–16 Aug 1762; 17 Aug 1762–Dec 1764. Gibbon was in Hampshire, with the militia, or in Paris, for most of this period, but he visited London on several occasions, and his social and professional activities there are clearly and fully described. BL Add MSS 37,722; 34,876

66. *1762* GREY, Jemima, *Marchioness Grey*, of Wrest Park, Beds. Diary of travel, including London, 1762–4. Beds RO L 30/9a/8

67. *1762* RANDALL, Richard, of Dulwich College, Organist and Fourth Fellow, schoolmaster. Diary, 1762–76, 1778–80, 1782–3, 1785. With much on his London activities and social life. Dulwich Coll 1632/3934–55

68. *1763* GRENVILLE, James, of Pinner, Middx. Diary, 1763–5, with daily observations on the natural and social life of Pinner, the weather, his garden, visits to the fair, horses, family, visitors, journeys to London and Stowe. Somerset ARS DD/S/BT 22/14

69. *1764* ANON, chaplain at a London hospital. Diary, 1764, daily life, with references to weather, expenses etc. Wales UL (Bangor) 2116 Bangor MSS

70. *1764* LEVELAND, Gervase, of London, son of woollen-draper. Lively social diary, July 1764–Oct 1765, about his travels around London and surrounding villages, friends, entertainments, flirtations. BL Add MSS 19211

71. *1764* MORGAN, John, of Pennsylvania, medical practitioner. Diary, 1764, of tour from Rome to London, people met, professional activities. Pennsylvania HS 431

72. *1765* BINYON, Edward, of Northampton, London draper's apprentice, Quaker. Diary, April 1765–Dec 1772. Life, worship, London sights. Wigan AS Mf 187

73. *1765* CULLEY, George, of Northumberland. Diary of travel, including London, 1765. Northumberland AS ZCU.1/1

74. *1765* FOLLIOTT, George, of America, merchant. Diary, Sept 1765–June 1766 of American colonist. Travel, business dealings in London, coffee houses, political and commercial contacts. Wigan AS EHC67/M836

75. *1765* WOIDE, Charles Godfrey, clergyman, orientalist and Biblical scholar, assistant librarian British Museum. Diary, 17 April 1765–6 May 1790, in German. His scholarly work, friends, social life and religious duties. BL Add MSS 48,700–5

76. *1768* THORNTON, John, of Clapham, trader. Diary for 1768 (Sundays only); and June–Dec 1768 (daily); and March–April 1779 (daily). Everyday events, and involvement with evangelical Clapham Sect. LMA ACC 2360/1–3

77. *1769* FOTHERGILL, Betty (Elizabeth), of Warrington, Quaker. Diary, 1769–70, of lengthy visit to London, staying with her uncle, Dr John Fothergill. Sightseeing, visits, shopping, excursions, social life and entertainment including the Lord Mayor's Show, as well as Quaker meetings. Lively style. There is a transcript. Friends' House MS Vol. S 51. MS Box 4 (8) – transcript

78. *1769* HUME-CAMPBELL, Amabel, *Baroness Lucas of Crudwell, Countess De Grey*, of Wrest, Beds, London, and Putney Heath. Diary, 1769–1827, of society life, including London seasons. W Yorks AS (Leeds branch) Vyner

79. *1770* JENKINS, James, of London, grocer, Quaker. Diary, Jan 1770–Jan 1831, covering his apprenticeship in Suffolk and his later career in Whitechapel. Reading, opinions, London scenes and activities. Friends' House Cupboard 5

80. *1770* WILKES, John, politician. Diary, from his release from King's Bench prison 17 April 1770–31 Oct 1797. Social and political activities, brief entries. Gordon riots. BL Add MSS 30,886

81. *1771* ANON, (male) of London, Baptist. Diary, 1771, kept by member of the Eagle Street meeting. Wesley Coll Bristol

82. *1771* MARCHANT, Henry, of Rhode Island, jurist. Copy of diary of voyage from Newport, RI to London, 1771–2, with descriptions of London and other cities. American Phil S B/M332

83. *1771* PARKE, Thomas, of Pennsylvania. Diary of voyage from Philadelphia to London, 1771–2. Pennsylvania HS 484a

84. *1771* PIGOTT, Nathaniel, of Brussels, astronomer, brother of Edward Pigott (**86**). Diary of his travels in 1771 including visiting friends in the London area and other social events, theatre visits, and management of his property at Whitton, Middx. Yale U Beinecke L Osborn Colln, fc 80

85. *1772* HUME-CAMPBELL, Alexander, *Lord Polwarth, Baron Hume of Berwick.* Diary of journeys from London to Scotland and back, 1772–4. Beds RO L 31/110

86. *1772* PIGOTT, Edward, astronomer, brother of Nathaniel Pigott (**84**). Diary, 1770–84, including visit to England, May–July 1772. Mentions visits to Ranelagh, Tower of London, Blackfriars Bridge, British Museum, Vauxhall and Greenwich as well as to the opera and the theatre. Yale U Beinecke L Osborn Colln, fc 80

87. *1772* POLHILL, Charles. Diary of a journey to London, Buckinghamshire and Oxfordshire, 1772. Kentish Studies U1007 F1

88. *1772* WOODS, Margaret, of Stoke Newington, Quaker. Diary, Jan 1772–June 1821. Religious life, reading, opinions, poetry. Extracts in *The Diary of Margaret Woods* (Philadelphia, 1850). Friends' House Box O

89. *1773* GIFFARD, Elizabeth, of Nerquis Hall, Flints. Diary of travel, including London, 1773. Flints RO D/NH/1076

90. *1773* RUDING, Rogers, receiver-general of Leicestershire. Diary, 1773–81, mainly relating to London business visits, but with some social notes. Leics RO 12D35

91. *1773* WARE, James, medical student. Diary, 1773–6 recording his medical studies, anatomy lectures, operations and his religious and social life in London. Surrey HC 1487/103/1–2

92. *1774* YEOMAN, John, of Hertfordshire. Modern extracts taken from his diary, 1774, recording his holiday experience around London. Herts ALS D/EBi.2/12

93. *1775* ANON. Diary of travel, including London, 1775. Shropshire RRC 2118/227

94. *1775* RICHARDSON, Dorothy, daughter of the Revd Henry Richardson, Rector of Thornton in Craven, Yorks. Diary, 1775 and 1785, of visits to London. John Rylands L English MS 1124

95. *1777* THORNTON, Henry, of London, banker and philanthropist. Diary, 1777–1815, which includes copies of family letters. Wigan AS D/DZ EHC18/ M786

96. *1781* GRIMSTON (née WALTER), Harriott, *Viscountess Grimston*, of Gorhambury, Herts, wife of 3rd Viscount Grimston. Diary, 1781–4. Herts ALS D/EV F39–42

97. *1782* JOHNSON, Samuel, lexicographer, biographer. Diary, 1782. Bodleian MS Don f. 6

98. *1782* WINDHAM, William, politician. Diary, 1782–1802, 'entirely distinct from the Diary of the Rt Hon William Windham (ed Mrs Baring, 1866)'. Notes on daily activities, travels, meetings. BL Add MSS 37,921–4

99. *1783* ENYS, John. Diary of journey including London, 1783. Cornwall RO EN 1806

100. *1783* SHOEMAKER, Samuel, Quaker, mayor of Philadelphia, loyalist refugee in London. Diary of his exile written 'for the entertainment of his wife', 1783–5. Pennsylvania HS 598

101. *1783* STANHOPE, *Sir* Henry Edwyn, *Bart*, of Stanwell House, Middx. Diary, 1783–1814. Huntington L Other Collns

102. *1785* CARTWRIGHT, Frances, of London. Diary and memoirs, 1785–1858, covering family life and travels. Notts Archives DD 1836

103. *1785* EYRE, Severn, of Eyre Hall, Virginia, medical student in London. Copy of diary, 1785–6, sent to his brother at home. Virginia HS MSS 5:1EY644:1

104. *1785* HOWARD, Charles, *11th Duke of Norfolk*. Diary, 1785–1815, of his private life, political and social activities. Cumbria RO D/HG1/1–9

105. *1786* COOPER, William, of Westminster Hospital, medical practitioner (student Assistant Physician or Surgeon). Diary, 1786, dealing with his medical studies but with much also on his leisure activities, pleasure trips, sport. Occasional shorthand passages. Wellcome MS 1856

106. *1787* HERVEY, Romaine, of Cambridge, clergyman. Transcript of a shorthand diary, covering visit to London in Feb 1787. Tourist sights, church-going. CUL Add 5944 (13)

107. *1788* BRAXTON, Carter, of Virginia. Diary, 1788–9, while in London and Brighton. Virginia HS MSS 5:1B7395:1

108. *1788* BURGESS, W Hugh, of St Marylebone, schoolboy. Diary, 1788–91, of a schoolboy living with parents and brothers. Social life, holidays, pets. Lively and informative about household routines. LMA F/WHB/1–3

109. *1788* GOFF, Elijah, of Stepney, coal merchant. Diary, 1788–99. Tower Hamlets LHLA TH/8383

110. *1788* JACKSON, Joseph, of Dublin, clergyman. Diary of a journey and visit to London, 1788. Nat L Ireland n.5731 p.6031

111. *1790* LARPENT (née PORTER), Anna Margaretta, wife of John Larpent, Examiner of Plays. Diary, 1790–1830, with gaps for 1801, 1819, 1822–3 and 1825. Domestic and theatrical events. Available on A Woman's View of Drama, 1790–1830 mf (Adam Matthew, 1995). Huntington L Other Collns

112. *1790* WIND, Paulus de. Journaal gehouden gedurende mijn verblijf te Londen, 1790–1. Daily notes on visit to London, attempts to make contact with medical world, operations at St Thomas's and Guy's hospitals. Zeeuwse B coll.hss. 6223 [In Dutch.]

113. *1791* HATFIELD, Mary, of Buxton. Travel diary, July–Aug 1791, including visit to London. John Rylands L English MS 1049

114. *1791* LEE, Philadelphia, of Totteridge Park, Herts. Diary, 1791–1811. Bucks RO D/LE/J1/11,12; AR 2/78

115. *1792* MARTIN-LEAKE, Mary, of Marshalls, Herts. Diary of travels, including London, 1792–1802. Herts ALS 84630

116. *1793* GILPIN, William, the younger, son of William Gilpin, author and clergyman. Diary, 1793–1847. Bodleian MS Eng. misc. f.201–350; f.351–60

117. *1793* GRAY, *Mr*, of London, Methodist. Diary, Dec 1793–Dec 1819, with notes of preachers and sermons, including London, and some family material. CUL Add MSS 6596

118. *1793* METCALFE, S, of Lincolnshire. Diary of travel, including London, 1793: the same tour as Mrs Monson (**119**). Lincs Archives MON 15/C/2

119. *1793* MONSON, *Mrs* William, of Burton, Lincs. Diary of travel, including London, 1793. Lincs Archives MON 15/C/1

120. *1793* PELHAM, Thomas, Member of Parliament for Sussex, later *2nd Earl of Chichester*. Diary, 30 Nov 1793–6 March 1794. Political manoeuvres surrounding Parliamentary support for the War, amid social life and personal problems at a critical time. Also upsetting death of his favourite dog. BL Add MSS 33,629–31

121. *1794* ANON, a member of the PLEYDELL BOUVERIE family. of Coleshill, Berks. Diary of journey from London to Edinburgh and back to Wiltshire, 1794. Berks RO D/EPb/F27

122. *1794* KEATE, Georgiana Jane, daughter of George Keate (author and painter), artist. Diary, 1794, 1802. Brief daily entries about family life, visits, friends, theatre going. Cultured circle, including Captain Bligh, artists, RSA luminaries. Daughter at home in 1794, by 1802 she was married to John Henderson, of the Adelphi, also an amateur artist. Private. Mrs S Bennett (susan@bennett.as) is preparing an edition for publication

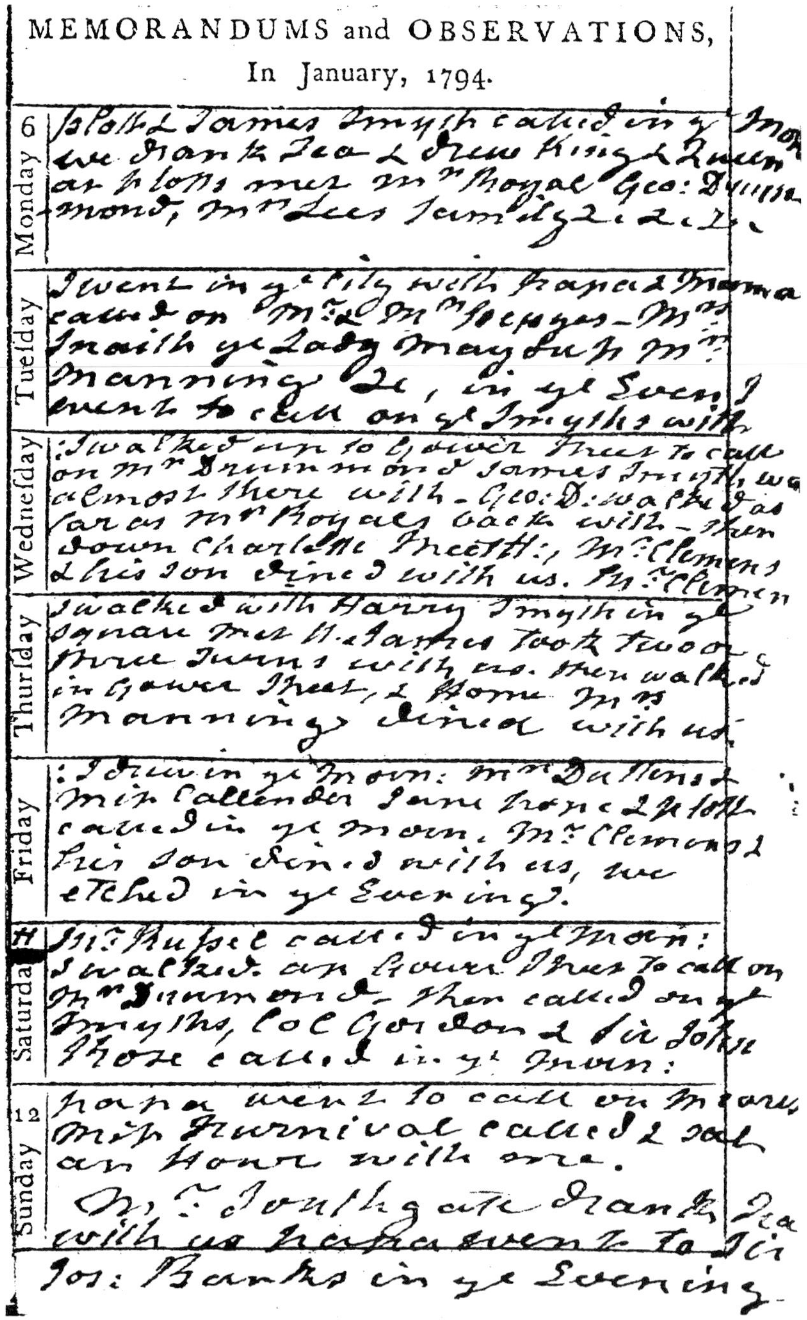

MEMORANDUMS and OBSERVATIONS,
In January, 1794.

6 Monday	Plott & James Smyth called in ye Morn we drank Tea & drew King & Queen at Plotts met Mr Royal Geo: Drummond, Mr Lees family &c. &c. &c.
Tuesday	I went in ye City with Papa & Mama called on Mr & Mrs Boggs—Mrs Smith ye Lady May but Mrs Manning &c, in ye Even I went to call on ye Smyths with
Wednesday	I walked up to Gower Street to call on Mr Drummond James Smyth, we almost there with Geo: D: walked as far as Mr Royals back with—then down Charlotte Street; Mr Clemens & his son dined with us. Mr Clemen
Thursday	I walked with Harry Smyth in ye Square met Miss Barnes took two or three Turns with us. then walked in Gower Street, & Home Mrs Manning dined with us.
Friday	I drew in ye Morn: Mr Dullens & Miss Callender Jane Rose & ye Plotts called in ye Morn. Mr Clemens & his son dined with us, we etched in ye Evening.
11 Saturday	Mr Russel called in ye Morn: I walked up Gower Street to call on Mr Drummond—then called on ye Smyths, Col Gordon & Sir John Rose called in ye Morn:
12 Sunday	Papa went to call on Mr [illegible] Miss Furnival called & sat an Hour with me. Mrs Southgate drank Tea with us Papa went to Sir Jos: Banks in ye Evening.

2. Georgiana Keate (**122**) describes her daily activities in early 1794 *(courtesy of Mrs S. Bennett)*

123. *1794* LLOYD, Thomas, radical, prisoner. Transcript of diary kept in Newgate Prison, 1794–6. An edition is in preparation for Leicester UP, by MT Davis and I McCalman. Philadelphia Arch HRC

124. *1794* RIDDELL, Elisa Ellery. Social diary, 1794, society, theatre, Hastings trial. Original in private hands. Yale UL mf 299

125. *1795* GUILLEBARD, *Mr.* Diary of journey from London to Cornwall and back, 1795. Cornwall RO AD 43

126. *1795* GODFREY, John W, of Pennsylvania. Diary of trip from Philadelphia to London on the brig *Diana*, and tour through England and continent, 1795–6. Pennsylvania HS 242

127. *1795* PLYMLEY, Katherine, of Longnor, Salop. Diary of travel, including London, 1795–6, 1813–14. Extract in *The Observant Traveller* (ed R Gard, 1989). Shropshire RRC 567/5/5/1/6–14, 28–32

128. *1796* ELPHINSTONE, Elizabeth Fullerton, of East Lodge, Enfield, wife of WF Elphinstone, a Director of the East India Company. Diary, 1796–1828, of life in Enfield and London. The series starts as 'journals of readings' with regular notes and criticisms of the books she is reading; from 1801 it is a mixture of reading and family life. BLOIO MSS. EUR F89 Box 1 (B) 16

129. *1797* HUNTER, Joseph, clergyman, antiquary, keeper of the Public Records. Diary of scholarly life, 3 March 1797–20 July 1799;21 April–23 May 1800;2 Jan 1806–28 Jan 1807;1808–14;11 Oct 1814–15 July 1819;21 April–17 June 1828;1833, 1841–60. And his 'thought-book',1826–59. Antiquarian pursuits in Bath and London, much in shorthand. BL Add MSS 24,879; 24,880; 24,441; 24,606; 24,446; 24,550–5; 33,601; 39,818–20

130. *1797* KIRK, Henry, of London, son of London merchant. Diary and autobiography, 15 July 1797–17 June 1818. In cipher, key available in volume. Public events, family affairs. BL Add MSS 37,326

131. *1797* SUTCLIFFE, John, of Halifax. Diary of visit to London, 1797. W Yorks AS (Halifax branch) HAS:681

132. *1797* SWETT, Mary Howell, Quaker. Diary of travels in England and continent, 1797–1801, including some time in London. Haverford Coll Quaker MS Colln 975C

133. *1798* BROUGHAM, Marianne, *Lady Brougham and Vaux*, of Brougham, Westmorland. Diary, 1798, 1806, 1809, 1815–63. First married to Thomas Spalding, her diary describes London social life until her husband's death in 1815; in 1819 she married the politician, Lord Brougham. UC London Brougham Papers

134. *1798* CATCHPOOL, John, of Tottenham, corn dealer, Quaker. Selections copied from his diary, May 1798–Dec 1846. Friends' House Box Y

135. *1798* SMITH, Charles Augustin, of Greenwich, solicitor. Diary, 1798–1838. Greenwich LHL Strongroom 1 G/13/B/34

136. *1798* KEVAN, Samuel, of Southwark (formerly of Wigtown), slater, and Reformed Presbyterian. Diary, 7 June 1798–19 May 1827. A good mix of work, personal life and religious activities. BL Add MSS 42,556

137. *1799* ANON, of London. Pocket diaries for 1799 and 1804 with brief notes on social life, theatregoing. Available on Women's Language and Experience mf pt 3 (Adam Matthew, 1999). CUL Add 7718–19

138. *1800* CULLUM, Susanna, of Hardwick, Suffolk. Diary of visit to London, Nov–Dec 1800. Available on Women's Language and Experience mf pt 3 (Adam Matthew, 1999). Suffolk RO (Bury) E2/44/66

139. *1800* GUEST, Rebecca, of Maryland. Copy of diary, 1800–10, kept while in England where her husband was head of merchant firm Guest & Co. Maryland HS MS 422

140. *1800* KING, Thomas, actor and dramatist. Diary, 1800, with notes of performances at Drury Lane and other memoranda including his ill-health. BL Add MSS 45,137

141. *1800* SHAEN (née SOLLY), Rebecca, of Walthamstow, Essex. Diary, 1800–55, of life in a lawyer's family. Bodleian MS MSS Johnson e.7

142. *1801* ANON. Diary of journey from London to Newcastle upon Tyne by sea, 1801. Cumbria RO (Kendal branch) WD/MG

143. *1801* FOX, George Townshend, of Westoe, South Shields, and Durham, rope-maker, later Deputy Lieutenant for Co Durham. Diary of his visits to London in 1801 and 1825. S Tyneside CL Fox Colln 120, 132

144. *1801* KNATCHBULL, *Sir* Edward, *9th Bart*, Paymaster-General. Diary of family events including deaths, 1801–46; political diaries, 1834–5, 1841–5, with notes added in 1846 and 1848. Kentish Studies F20, F21

145. *1801* MACKINTOSH, Catherine, *Lady Mackintosh*, wife of lawyer. Diary, Jan–July 1801. Lively entries about family life, dinner parties, amusements, visits to Vauxhall, French lessons. BL Add MSS 52450

146. *1801* WALDIE, John, of London. Diary, 1801–3, of family life, card games, theatre visits, music, literature. Yale UL Beinecke L d331

147. *1803* GILBERT, Mary Ann, of Cornwall. Diary, 1803–4, including time spent in London. Cornwall RO MSS DD EN.1917

148. *1803* GLYNNE, Mary, *Lady Glynne*, of Hawarden Castle, Flints, wife of Sir Stephen Glynne, 8th Bart, mother of Mary Glynne (**202**). Diary, 1803, 1804, 1819. St Deiniol's L MS 1062–5

149. *1803* UPCOTT, William, of London, bookseller, topographer. Diary, Jan 1803–7, on bookselling business, social life, theatregoing, personal affairs, health, reading; diary, 1809, 1823. Although this begins as a regularly kept diary, later entries appear more in the nature of memoirs, written after the events. BL Add MSS 32,558; UCL Ogden MSS 93

150. *1804* PLUMPTRE, James, Vicar of Great Gransden, Hunts, writer and clergyman. Diary, Jan 1804–Dec 1829, including occasional trips to London. His earlier journals appeared as James Plumptre's Britain: Journals of a Tourist in the 1790s (ed I Ousby, 1992). CUL Add MSS 5835–55

151. *1804* SMITH, Pleasance, *Lady Smith,* of Lowestoft, Suffolk, wife of founder of Linnean Society, botanist, and centenarian. Diary of a visit to London, 1804. Suffolk RO (Lowestoft) 12/1

152. *1805* FULLER, John, of Chesham, Bucks, and London. Diary, 11 Nov 1805–2 Dec 1807: 'I intend to keep a regular daily Journal of my studies, actions and opinions'. His social engagements, study and reading of the classics and the Bible, practising Italian, theatregoing. Wigan AS D/DZ EHC200/M1000

153. *1805* PENNANT, David, Snr, of Downing, Flints. Diary of travel, including London, 1805. Warwicks CRO CR.2119/F207

154. *1806* BOSWELL, James, junior, student at Brasenose College, Oxford. Diary, Jan.–Feb. 1806, covering visit to London. Brasenose MS 43

155. *1806* SCOTT, John Barber, of Bungay, Suffolk. Diary of a visit to London, 1806. Extracts in *The Englishman at Home and Abroad* (Ethel Mann, 1930). Suffolk RO (Lowestoft) 185/1/1

156. *1807* ATKINS, Samuel Elliott, of 6 Cowper's Court, Cornhill, Citizen and Clockmaker. Photocopy of diary, 1807, recording events mainly of family interest, with occasional entries on contemporary events. Guildhall L MS 15,819

157. *1807* EDGELL, Edgell Wyatt, of Milton Place, Egham, Justice of the Peace, landowner, father of Maria Frances Wyatt Edgell (**190**). Diary of his local activities in Surrey, but also visits to London to the theatre and opera, art sales, archaeological interests as well as family life. The diary covers 1807, 1810–11, 1812–15, 1816, 1818–19, 1835–8, 1840–5, 1847–49. Surrey HC 2088/1–7

158. *1807* GRENVILLE (née BRYDGES), Anna Eliza, *Duchess of Buckingham and Chandos,* wife of 1st Duke. Diary, 1807–34, with gaps. Huntington L Stowe Colln

159. *1807* ST GEORGE, Frances, wife of Colonel John St George (**160**). Diary, 1807–53. Southampton UL GB 0738 MS59

160. *1807* ST GEORGE, John, Army officer (Colonel), husband of Frances St George (**159**). Diary, 1807–53. Southampton UL GB 0738 MS59

161. *1807* WALKER, Anna, wife of Major-General George Townshend Walker. Mrs Walker's diaries run from 1789–1814 and deal mainly with travel and military postings, but she returned to England at intervals, including Feb–May 1807, and part of 1808, when she stayed near Kew and visited London, and Hampton Court. Wigan AS D/DZ EHC2/M770

162. *1808* ANON. Diary of a journey from Lancashire to London, *c.*1808. Lancs RO DDB 64/14

163. *1808* DULLES, Joseph, of Pennsylvania. Copy of diary, 1808–10, journey from New York to England, social, political and cultural life in London. Pennsylvania HS 179

164. *1808* ROWNTREE, Elizabeth, of Scarborough, Yorks, Quaker missionary, wife of shopkeeper. Diary, May 1808–Oct 1835, with many gaps. The writer lived in Scarborough, Yorks, but frequently visited London to attend Quaker meetings or visit Quaker families. Covers family life, bereavements, her religious work, travel, meals, people she met. Friends' House Box T

165. *1808* TYRRELL, Elizabeth senior and junior, wife and daughter of Timothy Tyrrell, City Remembrancer. Diary (photocopy) for periods between 1808 and 1822 by Elizabeth Tyrrell (1769–1835) and her daughter Elizabeth (b.1802). Vols. 1–2 (1808–11) are by Elizabeth senior, vols. 3–5 (1818–22) are by Elizabeth junior. Domestic life, family matters. Guildhall L MS 14,951/1–5

166. *1809* BEDINGFIELD (née JERNINGHAM), Charlotte, *Lady Beding-field*, of Oxburgh Hall, Norfolk, Woman of the Bedchamber to Queen Adelaide. Diary, 1809, 1816, 1818, 1819–20, 1830 (while at a convent in Hammersmith), 1831 and 1833 (at court). Available on Aristocratic Women mf pt 2 (Adam Matthew, 1998). Birmingham UL MS 82/1765–7; 1768–74

167. *1809* CHAMPION DE CRESPIGNY, Mary, of Champion Lodge, Denmark Hill, Camberwell, wife of Sir Claude Champion de Crespigny. Diary, 1809, social and family life. Yale U Beinecke L d 73 fd 44

168. *1809* GRIMSTON (née JENKINSON), Charlotte, *Countess of Verulam*, of Gorhambury, Herts, wife of 1st Earl of Verulam (**203**). Diary, including visits to London, 1809–14. Herts ALS D/EV F78

169. *1809* HOBHOUSE, *Sir* John Cam, later *Baron Broughton*, of Whitton, statesman. Diary, 1809–65. Lively, informal account of his daily activities. Travel, politics, dinner parties, theatre visits, social life, reformer's concerns, eg child prisoners in Newgate, 1818. Extracts in his *Memories of a Long Life* (1909). BL Add MSS 47,230 ff.41b, 127–57; 47,231–5

170. *1809* JENKINSON, *the Hon* Charles Cecil Cope, later *3rd Earl of Liver-pool*, statesman. Diary, March–July 1809, of personal and political life. Nat L Wales Pitchford Hall MS

171. *1810* VENN, Henry, clergyman, Secretary of the Church Missionary Society. Diary, 1810–73. Birmingham UL Special Collns

172. *1812* GRENVILLE, Richard, *2nd Duke of Buckingham and Chandos.* Diary, 1812, aged fifteen. Huntington L Stowe Colln

173. *1812* GRIMSTON, *the Hon* Charlotte, of Gorhambury, Herts, sister of Lord Verulam (**203**). Diary, 1812–24, 1826, 1828–9, of political and social events, including Thames frost fair, 1814. Herts ALS D/EV F81–96

3. Raleigh Trevelyan (**176**) tries to see the visiting Tsar of Russia in 1814 *(courtesy of Wigan Archives Service)*

174. *1813* HOLTZAPFEL, Charlotte, of Clements Lane, Cockspur Street, daughter of, and wife of, City businessmen. Diary, 11 Aug 1813–16, 1817–20, 1824–36, covering middle class social activities, concerts,exhibitions; marriage to William Boycott, childbirth, family life, health worries, medical treatment. Wigan AS D/DZ EHC122/M890;134/M902

175. *1813* LETTSOM, John Coakley, medical practitioner. Diary, 1 Jan 1813–31 Dec 1814, concentrating on personal rather than professional life. And the weather. Extracts in *Lettsom: his Life, Times, Friends and Descendants* (ed JJ Abraham, 1933). Wellcome Medical SL

176. *1813* TREVELYAN, Raleigh, schoolboy. Diary, 15 April 1813–11 July 1814, kept while at school with his brother at the Revd Mr Morris's Academy, Egglestone House, Brentford, with holidays in London and Ramsgate. Family activities, Tsar's visit in 1814, unhappy schooldays, treatment for his failing health, his fatal illness. Wigan AS D/DZ EHC191/M983

177. *1813* WARD, James, painter. Diary, 1813–26, of his painting and social life. R Academy

178. *1814* ANON, a member of the STRUTT family, *Barons Belper*, of Belper, Derbys. A diary of travel, including London, 1814–15, 1831. Derbys RO D2943M/F1/1–2; F2/1

179. *1814* ABBOTT, later COLFOX, Hannah, of Bridport, Dorset. Diary of London visits, March–June 1814, and 1818–19. Dorset RO D 43/F11, F15

180. *1814* LINDSAY, *Lady* Charlotte, sister of 5th Earl of Guilford. Diary, 1814, and 18 April–31 Dec 1840. Weather, often including temperature, social engagements, fellow dinner guests. Her reading. West End society life. Bodleian MS Eng. misc. 226; BL Sheffield Park papers Add MSS 61,987

181. *1814* OGDEN, William Bernard, of Durham. Diary of life in Durham and London, 1814–22. Durham CRO D/X 782/1–4

182. *1814* RUSSELL, Fanny, of Cornwall. Diary of visit to London, 1814. Cornwall RO HL(2)379

183. *1815* BARNES, Robert, of North London, Enfield area. Diary, 1815–58. Brief daily notes of family activities around Enfield, Edmonton, Tottenham and Mill Hill with occasional visits to central London. Earliest years are more detailed about daily life in London. For most years, also a separate, fuller account of the family seaside holiday at various Kent and Sussex resorts. Many ephemera included. LMA ACC 69.084

184. *1815* BODDINGTON, Samuel, of London, fishmonger. Diary, 1815–43, covering social and family life, and travels. Guildhall L MS 10,823/5c

185. *1815* MINET, James Lewis, of London, merchant. Diary, 1815–20, from the ages of sixteen to twenty-one. Huguenot L F Mt 229

186. *1815* MUCKLESTONE-ALLEN, David, of London, son of businessman. Diary, 1815. Yale UL 43.341–2

187. *1815* VENN, Emelia, of London. Diary, 1815–32, including travel and home life. Birmingham UL Venn MSS 19–21

188. *1816* BATTEY, Charles, of Hanwell, parish clerk. Diary, 1816–59, brief entries about sporting and social events, local news and parish business. Ealing LHL

189. *1817* DE COETLOGON, Charles Frederick, of Ashford, and St George Hanover Square, writer and clergyman. Diary, 1817, 1828. Daily routine, domestic incidents, visits, correspondence, health, weather. Other volumes do not relate to London. LMA ACC 268/1, 7

190. *1817* EDGELL, Maria Frances Wyatt, of Milton Place, Egham, and Grosvenor Street, daughter of Edgell Wyatt Edgell (**157**). Diary, 1817, 1841, 1852–3, 1855–7, 1862, 1868–9, 1872. The earliest diary records a visit to London with full round of social engagements including balls and the theatre. By 1841 she had settled in London, records domestic life, visits, local charity work (including Hanover Square district schools), lectures, theatre, art galleries, visits to her brother who was rector of North Cray. Surrey HC 2088/ 3,7,8; 4190

191. *1817* EMLEN, Samuel, of the United States. Diary, 1817–18, living in England with invalid wife, including some visits to London. Haverford Coll Quaker MS Colln 975B

192. *1817* GIDEON, *Miss* E A, of Paddington. Diary, 1817–18. Available on Women's Language and Experience mf pt 3 (Adam Matthew, 1999). Suffolk RO (Ipswich) HD 298/1–2

193. *1817* HILL, Matthew Davenport, prison reformer. Diary, 1817–18, about personal and social life, his work, visits to London. Bodleian MS Eng. Misc. e.88

194. *1817* JOHNSTON, Jane, of Wimpole Street, widow. Diary, 1817, 1819–40, of engagements, household and personal expenditure, health, family life. Herts ALS 16195–16217

195. *1818* ANON, (male) of London. London diary and commonplace book, July 1818–Dec 1824, mentioning sporting events, theatre, court, gossip. Civic life of City. Guildhall L MS 3730

196. *1818* ANON, (male) of Edinburgh. Diary, 1818, covering visit to London. Nat L Scotland MS 166

197. *1818* ARROWSMITH (née LEE), Louisa, of Totteridge Park, Herts. Diary, 1818–26, 1827–32, 1836–7, relating to town and country life, gardens, journeys, contemporary events. Available on Women's Language and Experience mf pt. 1 (Adam Matthew, 1996). Herts ALS 70150–68

198. *1818* BANKS, John Cleaver, of London. Diary, 1818, with brief entries relating to his financial dealings, reading, social engagements and church going. Wigan AS D/DZ EHC65/M834

199. *1818* HUXTABLE, Elizabeth, of Devon. Typed copy of a diary describing a visit to London, April 1818–April 1819. Theatre visits, scientific lectures, social engagements, tourist sights, Lord Mayor's Show. With the diary is a brief transcript extract from the diary of Mary Huxtable, a relative, who visited London 1820–1, calling at the Royal Society of Arts and the Royal Institution. Whereabouts of original is unknown. Bishopsgate I L17

200. *1818* KNIGHT, Job, of St Martin's, Ludgate, cabinet maker, Quaker. Diary, 1818, with much on his daily work, journeys around London and Quaker meetings. Friends' House MS Vol. S 485

201. *1819* CHURCHILL, Charles, senior and junior, of Churchill & Sim, wood brokers. Diary by Charles Churchill, senior (d. 1844) and Charles Churchill, junior (d. 1905). Entries relate to the timber trade, City politics and private affairs. Vols. 1–22 by CC senior, 1819–44; vols. 23–63 by CC junior, 1841–1904. Guildhall L MS 5762/1–63

202. *1819* GLYNNE, Mary, of Hawarden Castle, Flints, daughter of Mary, Lady Glynne (**148**). Diary, 1819. St Deiniol's L MS 1120

203. *1819* GRIMSTON, James Walter, *4th Viscount Grimston, 1st Earl of Verulam*, of Gorhambury, Herts, husband of Charlotte Grimston (**168**), and brother of the Hon Charlotte Grimston (**173**). Diary, 1819–29, 1832. Some coverage of London season. Herts ALS D/EV F44

204. *1819* MADDEN, *Sir* Frederic, Keeper of Manuscripts, British Museum. Diary, 1819–72. Bodleian MS Eng. hist. *c.*140–82

205. *1819* O'DONOVAN, Richard, Army officer (Major-General, 6th Dragoons). Diary, 1819–23, including visits to London, and his farming activities. Bath CL Nos.1253–4

206. *1820* ANON, of Sheffield, medical student. Diary, Sept 1820– June 1821, about his medical training in London, student life, Unitarian interests. Chetham A.3.108

207. *1820* CHORLEY, Eleanor, of Congleton, Cheshire. Diary, 1820–50, including visits to London. Cheshire CALSS D 4806

208. *1820* NEWMAN, William, of Stepney. Diary, 1820–5. Baptist life and work in East London. Regent's PC Angus Lib

209. *1820* TREVELYAN, Julia, of Bath. Diary, 1820, including a visit to London. Somerset ARS DD/WO/54/11/24

210. *1821* BLAKE, John, of Park Lane, Croydon, auctioneer. Diary, 1821–40, including copies of correspondence with friends and relatives. Croydon LSL Acc 483

211. *1821* HOWARD, Henry, of Penrith, Cumberland. Diary of travel from London to Lake District, 1821. Cumbria RO D/HW8/5

212. *1822* ANON. Diary of a visit to London, 1822. Yale U Beinecke L d312

213. *1822* BRANFILL, Eliza, of Upminster, Essex. Diary, 1822–72. Essex RO MSS D/DRU F12/1–45

214. *1822* BRINKLEY, Sarah, of Fortland, Co Sligo, Ireland. Diary of travel, including London, 1822. Denbighs RO (Ruthin branch) DD/PR/133

215. *1822* GRAY, Margaret, of Gray's Court, York. Diary, 1822, 1823–5, including visits to London. N Yorks CRO ZGY/T8

216. *1823* COTTON, H S, clergyman, chaplain at Newgate Prison. Diary and visiting book, 1823, of his daily visits to the prison, conversations with prisoners, executions. Australian NL MS 14

217. *1823* FRASER, Jane Satchell, wife of Edward Satchell Fraser. Diary (photocopy), 1823, of London social life, daily activities, family, church going, servant problems. A difficult hand. BLOIO Photo.Eur. 172

218. *1823* GLADSTONE, Catherine, of Hawarden Castle, Flints, mother of Henry Neville Gladstone (**443**). Diary, 1823–30, 1840–62. St Deiniol's L MS 1764–71

219. *1823* GRENVILLE, Richard, *1st Duke of Buckingham and Chandos*. Personal and political diary, 1823. Huntington L Stowe Colln

220. *1823* HARDING, James Duffield, of Barnes, watercolour artist. Diary, 1823–63. Courtauld CI/JDH

221. *1823* NICHOLS, Mary Anne Iliffe, of Hampstead, Westminster, Clapham and Hammersmith, daughter of John Bowyer Nichols, printer and antiquary. Diary, 1823–34. c/o Surrey HC Julian Pooley, Nichols Archive Project

222. *1823* SHORT, *Mr*, of Kenn, Devon. Diary of travels on the Grand Tour, with detailed description of London and other cities, 1823–4. Devon RO MSS 1311 M/6/13

223. *1823* WOLLEY, Thomas Lamplugh, of Clifton, Bristol, son of Mr Wolley (**235**). Diary, including a visit to London in Aug–Sept 1823 en route to Germany. While in London he dined with the Duke of Clarence and the Duchess of Saxe-Weimar. LMA ACC 0611/2

224. *1824* BARRETT, Betsy, of Leeds. Diary of young married woman's visit to London, May–June 1824, to stay with relations. Extensive sightseeing, theatregoing, shopping, Vauxhall Gardens and other diversions. Extracts in *London Topographical Record*, XXVIII (2001). E R Yorks A DDX/94/190

225. *1824* CAPPER, later HARDCASTLE, Anne, of Stoke Newington, schoolgirl, Quaker. Diary, 1824–30, begun as a child of seven. Domestic life, lessons, excursions with parents or governess, family visitors, her pets, holidays. Lord Mayor's Show. Antislavery meetings, lectures. Available on Quaker Women's Diaries mf (World Microfilms Pubns, 1978). Friends' House Temp. MSS 310/1–3

226. *1824* TURNER, *Lady*, of Kirkleatham Hall, Yorks. Diary, 1824–5, mainly about the London season. N Yorks CRO Kirkleatham Hall 11782–5

227. *1825* CARTWRIGHT-DENT, *Mr*, of Burlington Street. Diary, 1825. Plymouth and W Devon RO 551/1

228. *1825* COOPER, Anthony Ashley, *7th Earl of Shaftesbury*, philanthropist. Diary, social life and politics, 1825–85. Southampton UL SHA/PD/1–12

229. *1825* DORVILLE, Anne, of Clapham, servant or companion. Diary 1825–37, domestic and religious matters, some holidays. In 1833 she moved to Hammersmith alone after the death of her mistress from cholera. Bodleian MS Eng. misc. d.352

230. *1825* GRENVILLE (née CAMPBELL), Mary, *Duchess of Buckingham and Chandos*, wife of 2nd Duke. Diary, 1825–39, 1844–6. Huntington L Stowe Colln

231. *1825* ISHAM, *Sir* Justinian, *8th Bart*, of Lampton Hall, Northants. Diary, 1825–43, including London visits. Northants RO Isham 20

232. *1825* ST GEORGE, *Sir* John, Army officer (General), son of John and Frances St George (**159, 160**). Diary, 1825–91. Southampton UL GB 0738 MS59

233. *1826* ANON. Diary of travels, including London, 1826–38. Norfolk RO MS80 T 131 C

234. *1826* CONGREVE, Harriet Frances, of Congreve, Staffs. Diary of a visit to London, 1826. Staffs RO D1057/P/4

235. *1826* WOLLEY, *Mr*, of Clifton, father of Thomas Lamplugh Wolley (**223**). Diary, March–July 1826 covers a visit to London before his final illness and death. LMA ACC 0611/5

236. *1827* LAPIDGE, Charles H, of Hampton Wick, retired RN officer, uncle of Marianne Lapidge (**269**). Diary, Feb 1827–March 1829. Domestic activities. Mentions opening of Kingston upon Thames Bridge, 1828. His brother Edward was its architect. Wigan AS EHC70/M839;119/M887

237. *1827* MORAN, Edward Raleigh, journalist, of *The Globe*. Diary, mainly about his life in Dublin, but including two busy visits to London, 1827 and 1830–1. BL Egerton 2156

238. *1827* SPURRETT, Eliza, of Leicestershire. Diary of visits to London, 1827, 1839, 1846. Leics RO 7D54/2/2–4

239. *1828* GLADSTONE, *Sir* Thomas, of Hawarden Castle, Flints. Diary, 1828, 1843. St Deiniol's L MS 1291–2

240. *1828* GODLEE, Mary, of Upton, and Whipps Cross, Quaker. Diary, 1828–38, 1841, 1846, begun when she was a schoolgirl. Domestic life, holiday trips. Friends' House MS Vol. S 497–500

241. *1828* ROBERTS, James Austin, Congregational minister. Diary, 1828–62, of self and other members of family. Bodleian MS Eng. Misc. e. 996–1009

242. *1828* THORNHILL, John, Director of East India Company. Diary, 1828–40, with day to day household accounts. Barclays

243. *1828* WOOLCOTT, George, of London, evangelist. Diary, *c.*1828. Nat Maritime M X96/035

244. *1829* HEKEKYAN BEY, Joseph, Egyptian Armenian archaeologist and administrator. Diary, July 1829–Jan 1830, 16 May–22 Oct 1862, while in England. London friends, visits, scholarly meetings, sightseeing – Crystal Palace, British Museum, Soane Museum (in 1862). Extracts in *Victorian Diaries* (ed H Creaton, 2001). BL Add MSS 37,448; 37,456

245. *1829* LE GRICE, Charles Valentine, humorist and writer. Diary of travel, including London, 1829. Cornwall RO X 30/41

246. *1830* ROUMIEU, John F, of London. Diary, 1830–2, of life and society in London. Derbys RO 104M/E71–4

247. *1831* ANON, (male) of the United States, traveller. Diary, 1831, of American's European tour, including a visit to London. New York PL

248. *1831* HALE, Robert Hale Blagden. Memo book including diary entries for a visit to London in June 1831 and two visits in 1832. Glos RO D 1086/F 172

249. *1831* HALFORD, *Sir* Henry, *Bart*, of Mayfair, and Wistow Hall, Leics, medical practitioner (physician). Diary, 1831–4, of professional and social life. Leics RO DG 24

250. *1831* HOOK, Theodore, of Hammersmith, playwright and novelist. Mid-19th century copy of section of his diary, March 1831–Jan 1832, the location of the original is unknown. Hammersmith ALHC DD/763

251. *1831* LISTER, Anne, of Shibden Hall, Halifax. Diary, 1819–39, of travel, including nineteen visits to London. Social and personal details, topographical descriptions, visits to opera, diorama, zoo, Thames tunnel. Some sections in code. W Yorks AS (Halifax branch) SH:7/ML/TR/11

252. *1831* PETHERAM [?], John, clerk and member of the City of London Scientific Institution. Diary, 1831–2, of his social life, opinions on books and sermons. A later volume deals with his life in New York. He was probably John Petheram, author and publisher (d. 1854). Bodleian MS Lyell Empt. 38

253. *1831* STEWART, Alvan, of New York. Diary of trip to England, 1831. New York HS

254. *1831* TAYLOR, Daniel Carrington, of New York, traveller. Diary of European tour, 1831, including London. New York HS

255. *1832* ANON, (male) of London. Diary, 1832–8, in Harding's shorthand. U London L Carlton MS 17/7

256. *1832* BAKER, Caroline Julia, wife of Colonel George Baker. Diary, 1832–6, including time spent in London. Bodleian MS Dep.e.60–4

257. *1832* DENMAN, Frances, of Russell Square, daughter of Lord Chief Justice Denman. Diary, 1 July 1832–23 April 1833, including life in Russell Square, with descriptions of her domestic activities, social engagements, and political news. Wigan AS D/DX EHC183/M975

258. *1832* HUNTER, John Charles, of 30 Wilton Place, Knightsbridge, medical practitioner. Diary, 24 Nov 1832–26 Feb 1836, 9 Oct 1833–22 Dec 1834, 13 Nov 1843–13 April 1852. Personal and family life, sermons heard, some mention of patients. Filled in from each end of same volume. A difficult hand. WCA Ac 182/4

259. *1832* ROWSELL, William. Diary, 1832–3, about daily life and work, and preparations for emigration to Canada. He worked in the family stationery firm in Cheapside. Guildhall L MS 24,458

260. *1832* SANDS, W [?], of Atherstone, Warwicks. Travel diary, begins April 1832, with visit to London. Birmingham CA IIR11 (259856)

261. *1832* SIDDONS, Henry, son of Henry Siddons, actor-manager. Diary, 1830–3. Nat L Scotland Acc 5731

262. *1833* ANON, of Hull. Diary, 22 Jan–9 Sept 1833, of young girl – possibly a relation of William Etty, the painter. Diary covers travels, including a visit to London, staying in Clapham and Blackheath, when she saw the House of Commons, National Gallery, Westminster Bridge, and several dioramas. Wigan AS EHC96/M864

263. *1833* BELDAM, Valentine. Diary of a journey including London, 1833. IOW CRO IW/99

264. *1833* BUDDLE, John, of Co Durham, mining engineer. Diary of visit to London, 1833. Durham CRO D/X 563/1

265. *1833* BURTON, Charles, of Hanwell, schoolboy. Diary, 1833–4, of life at Hanwell Academic Institution: lessons, excursions, routine activities, little comment. Ealing LHL 210/1–3

266. *1833* COOPER, James Fenimore, of the United States, novelist. Travel diary, June–Sept 1833, kept in London. Yale UL

267. *1833* HOFFMAN, David, of Baltimore, lawyer. Diary of European tour with his family, including six weeks in London, 1833. Visits to Court, opera, theatre, concerts, King's Bench. New York PL

268. *1833* HUDLESTON, Andrew Fleming, of Rydal, Cumberland, East India Company tax collector and magistrate. Diary, 1833, covering his arrival back in London in ill-health after Indian service. Cumbria RO DHud/3/5/3

269. *1833* LAPIDGE, Marianne, of Hampton Wick, Middx, schoolgirl, niece of Charles H. Lapidge (**236**). Diary, 1 Jan–21 Dec 1833 describing domestic life and music lessons. Wigan AS EHC72/841

270. *1833* LAYCOCK, Thomas, medical practitioner (Professor of the Practice of Physic, Edinburgh University). Diary, 1833–57, including time as medical student in London. Edinburgh UL Gen 1813

271. *1833* SELOUS, H C, painter of panoramas. Diary, 1833–4, of his life and work in London. Catalogued as 'Journal kept by an unknown painter of panoramas', but identified by Mr R Hyde as Selous. Nat Art L 86.SS.67

272. *1834* ADAMS, E Richards, of Elmer Lodge, Beckenham, Kent, solicitor. Diary, 1834–8, of family and personal events, church affairs, travel. Some shorthand. Bromley AS MSS. Acc.789.

273. *1834* ALDAM, William, of Doncaster, Member of Parliament. Diary of travel, including London, 1834, 1840. Doncaster Archives DD/WA

274. *1834* ANON, (male) of London. Domestic diary, Nov 16 1834–Sept 3 1836. A further volume deals with a trip to Germany. In London the author was a keen theatre and operagoer (e.g. *I Puritani*), a family man, with an interest in current events and cultural matters. Sees Jeremy Bentham's 'reliques', art exhibition at Somerset House. Wigan AS D/DX EHC22/M790

275. *1834* LONGMAN, H, of Sheepcote Farm, Harrow, farmer. Diary, 1834–5. Mainly agricultural matters, but includes visits to London and details of loads of produce sent in. Harrow LHC D2a Oversize

276. *1834* MARRIOT, J. Diary entitled 'A journey to London with S A Marriot in search of health, accompanied by Louisa and Margaret in search of pleasure, and followed by Tom Hobson in search of his wife', 8–27 Oct 1834. The party travelled to London by canal boat from Runcorn. On arrival they visited the sights, and describe the Houses of Parliament on fire. Wigan AS EHC197/M998

277. *1834* PUGH, Charles, of Barnard's Inn, clerk in High Court of Chancery. Diary, 1834–63. Bodleian MS Eng. misc. d.465–73

278. *1834* RODD, Francis, of Trebartha, North Hill, Cornwall, retired Army officer (Colonel). Diary, kept in London, 1834. Cornwall RO MSS ADD 360/23

279. *1834* STEVENSON, Arthur, Heath keeper on Hampstead Heath. Record book and diary, 1834–49. Camden LSAC D/57 (fiche)

280. *1835* BENSON, Samuel, clergyman, Vicar of St Saviour's, Southwark. Diary, 1835–78, with gaps. Bodleian MS Eng. misc. e.527–35

281. *1835* DIGBY (née FOX-STRANGWAYS), Theresa Anna, Woman of the Bedchamber, wife of 9th Baron Digby. Diary, 1835–8. Barings 136

282. *1835* GOSLING, Francis, of London. Diary of voyage from London to Sydney, 1835, starting with travel on the steamer Mercury to Gravesend. Nat Maritime M MS ALE <147191>

283. *1835* RICHARDSON, Charles, civil engineer, pupil of Brunel. Diary, 1835–8, of his work with Brunel and his life in general. Enthusiastic gymnast, swimmer and rower. In London at some stage each year. Private. Being edited for an MPhil. by Peter Griffin, Gloucester U

284. *1836* POLHILL, Frances M, of Howbury Hall, Beds, wife of Member of Parliament. Diary, 1836, takes children to London sights, and to church. Theatre visits, painting exhibitions. Domestic affairs, her own serious illness. Herts ALS D/P 78 29/1

285. *1836* REES, William, of Llandovery, Carm, printer and bookseller. Diary, 1836, 1855, 1857, 1859–61, 1866–9, 1871. Business life and local events, with visits to London and other places. Crystal Palace. Cardiff CL 2.647

286. *1837* ANON, a member of the CLOVER family, of Norfolk. Diary of visits to London, May–June 1837 and April–May 1859. Norfolk RO MS 21842 MC 115/5, 8

287. *1837* BACON, Jane Margaret, of Cambridge. Diary, 1837–70, brief notes of social life and activities, frequent visits to London. Available on Women's Language and Experience mf pt 3 (Adam Matthew, 1999). CUL Add 6253

288. *1837* ROGERS, Ann S C, wife of J E Thorold Rogers, mother of Clement F Rogers (**496**). Diary, 1837–98. Bodleian MS Eng. misc. g.100/ 1–18; g.101/1–15; f.479–94

289. *1837* ROTHSCHILD, *Lady* Louisa de, philanthropist. Diary, 29 July 1837–2 Dec. 1907, with gaps, of family life in London, court life, music, travel, sport. BL Add MSS 47,949–62

290. *1838* HALL, Emily and Ellen, of West Wickham, Kent, sisters of Louisa Sherrard (**401**). Diary, 1838–1901. Lived in West Wickham from 1842, both wrote lively accounts of their activities, health, thoughts and feelings for nearly 60 years. Much Continental travel, visits to North Africa, frequently stayed in London. Extracts in *Two Victorian Girls* (OA Sherrard, 1964); *The Halls of Ravenswood*, and, *Two Victorian Ladies* (AR Mills, 1967, 1969) and *Vanished West Wickham* (J Waller, 1994). Bromley AS MS 855

291. *1838* PARKINSON-FORTESCUE, Chichester Samuel, *2nd Baron Carlingford*, statesman. Diary, 1838–98. Political matters, dinner parties, London social life, the weather. Touching description of his grief at his wife's death in 1879. BL Add MSS 63,654–704

292. *1838* —, Thomas, footman, in service with the 2nd Duke of Sutherland. Diary, including life in the Leveson-Gower household at Stafford House, London, 1838–9. Staffs RO 4177/1–2

293. *1839* BRYDGES, John, of Tibberton, Herefs. Diary of a journey including London, 1839. Hereford RO K12/99

294. *1839* JONES, Ernest Charles, Chartist politician, poet, novelist. Diary, July 1839–May 1847. Social and working life, Chartist politics. Manchester LSAC BR MSS 932 2 J 18

295. *1839* PHILIPPS, Eliza, *Lady Philipps*, later *Baroness Milford*, of Picton Castle, Pembs. Diary, 1839–44, including daily life in London, in Portland Place. Social life, family health, and political news. Domestic arrangements including hiring and firing servants. Nat L Wales Picton Castle 607

296. *1839* POHLMAN, Robert Williams, of London, emigrant to Australia. Photocopied diary, 1839–55, the first volume of which describes his life in London before emigrating. State L Victoria

297. *1839* WOOD, Thomas Peploe, of Great Haywood, Staffs, artist. Diary, 1839–44, including visits to London. Staffs RO MS

298. *1840* DE LISLE (née CLIFFORD), Laura, of Quenby Hall, Leics. Diary, 1840–96. Life in a prominent Catholic family, with frequent trips to London, eg to see the Great Exhibition in 1851. Private. With the family at Quenby Hall, Leics.

299. *1840* GREW, Mary, of Philadelphia, abolitionist. Diary, 1840, covering the World Anti-Slavery Convention in London from which she and other female delegates were excluded. Radcliffe I M–59 reel 973 no.M13

300. *1840* GRIFFITH, Charles James, emigrant to Australia. Photocopied diary, begun in London in 1840, going on to describe his voyage to Australia and life there. State L Victoria

301. *1840* HUNTER, Fredericka Emma, *Lady Hunter*. Diary, 1840–6. The Hunters had a house in Brighton, but spent the season in London. Social life, reading, visits, theatre, art exhibitions. Frequent references to 'dear Sir Richard', her husband. Possibly written for general family consumption. WCA Acc 1621

302. *1840* NEVILL (née WALPOLE), *Lady* Dorothy Fanny, hostess, horticulturalist. Diary, social and personal, 1840–5. Lewis Walpole L

303. *1840* ROGERS, Thomas, London partner of Nottingham firm Rogers & Co, hosiery manufacturers. Diary, 1840–98, chiefly personal and domestic matters. He was a liveryman of the Broderers' Company, and a talented amateur musician. Drawings of comets he saw in 1848 and 1861. Guildhall L MS 19,019

304. *1840* TAYLOR, Sophia, later *Mrs* Thomas Edward COOKE, of Adelaide. Diary, 1840–2, kept in London before she emigrated. State L S Australia D 6846(L)

305. *1841* PASLEY, *Sir* Charles William, Army officer (Major-General, Royal Engineers). Pasley spent much of his career abroad, and his diaries run from 1799–1848. London interest is concentrated in the years 1841–6 when he was Inspector General of Railways. Coverage includes his official duties, and distress when dismissed from the post, but also London social and family life. BL Add MSS 41,977–8; 41,983–92

306. *1842* CAPELL, *Lady* Adela, of Eglinton Castle, Ayrs, daughter of 6th Earl of Essex. Diary 1841–2, including a visit to London in 1842 at age of fourteen. Social life, pets. Herts ALS D/Z 32 F1

307. *1843* GYE, Frederick, the younger, Director of the Italian Opera. Diary, 1843–78, dealing with Vauxhall Gardens, Covent Garden and Drury Lane theatres. An edition is in preparation by M. Ringel and F. Franchi. R Opera House

308. *1842* LYALL, Charles, of London, banker, partner in Lyall, Matheson & Co. Diary begins in 1828 in India; in 1842 he returned to live in Westbourne Terrace, Hyde Park. Domestic and family life, business in City. BLOIO MS.EUR. C209/1–67

309. *1843* HOLYOAKE, George Jacob, co-operator and secularist. Diary, 1845, 1849, 1850, 1853–63, 1865–7, 1879–81, 1882–1905, and diary notebook 1847–52. Bishopsgate I Holyoake Papers 9, 10, 16

310. *1844* ANON, of Shoreditch area. Diary and notebook, 1844–55, in a diary for 1839. Hackney AD M4233/1

311. *1843* SCOTT, Jessy Emma, of Ravenscourt. Photocopy of diary ('Journal Book V'), Dec 1843–Aug 1844. Hammersmith ALHC DD/272

312. *1844* BLACK, William Henry, of Goodman's Fields, later of Mill Yard Meeting House, Whitechapel, antiquary, Assistant Keeper of the Public Records. Diary, 1844–6, personal life, work at the PRO and his historical research. Chetham Mun A.2.111

313. *1844* BOUSTEAD, John, of 8 Upper Gloucester Place, Army agent, of Price & Boustead, 33–34 Strand. Rough entries 4 July–22 Nov 1844, and diary, 1 Aug 1855–18 Jan 1861. He had served as a regimental paymaster in Ceylon before retirement. WCA Acc 950

314. *1844* COOK (née BICKERSTETH), Harriet, religious writer, wife of WH Cook, MD, sister of Charlotte Bickersteth (**376**). Diary, 1844–1915, of her life in London, family illnesses, religious feelings and duties. Wellcome PP/COO/H1–62

315. *1844* DELARUE, J Ludlow, schoolmaster, later of Lancing College. Diary, 1844, while living in London as a young man. Birmingham UL MS 26

316. *1844* GORDON, Maria Antonietta, *Marchioness of Huntly*, of Orton Hall, Peterborough, botanist. Diary, 1844–93. Though much of her time was spent in the country, she made frequent visits to London in her younger years, for shopping, finding servants, visiting friends and family, and for the social season. Extract in *London Topographical Record*, XXVIII (2001). Huntingdon CRO 539/1–16

317. *1844* HANSARD, Luke Henry, son of Luke Hansard, parliamentary printer. Diary, 1844–51. Southampton UL GB 0738 MS59

318. *1844* RYDE, Edward, of Warwick Square and Woking, surveyor. Diary, 1844–92, of a pioneering professional surveyor and valuer. His travelled widely for his work, but lived and/or worked in London throughout his career. Close family life, and professional activities. Surrey HC 1262/1/28–49

319. *1844* SEYMOUR, Adelaide Horatia, later second wife of Frederick, 4th Earl Spencer. Diary, 28 Sept–10 Oct 1844, 19 June 1845–8 March 1846 of a young girl's visits, amusements, balls, dancing partners, social events in royal circles. BL Add MSS 62,914–15

320. *1844* SILVESTER, Thomas Hookham, founder of Clapham General Dispensary. Notebook containing diary and other memoranda on his financial affairs, investments, legacies, and patients, 1844–76. The diary section intermingles his private life and his medical duties. Wellcome MS 5869

321. *1844* STEVENS, William, of Fleet Street. Diary, 1844–5, reflecting his scientific and cultural interests: engraving, photography, astronomy, optical glass, mathematics and music. UC London MS Ogden 89

322. *1844* TARLETON (née DIMSDALE), Finetta Esther. Diary, 1844–5, 1852, about social life in London and Hertfordshire. Liverpool RO Tarleton papers MSS 184–5

323. *1845* COBB, Thomas Pix, of Janson, Cobb, Pearson & Co, solicitor. Diary with personal expenses, and notes about private, business and public occasions, 1845–56. Guildhall L MS 18,770/1–11

324. *1845* LAMBERT, Annie, of 33 Tavistock Square, London, daughter of wine merchant. Diary, Jan–July 1845. Home and social life, shopping, entertainment. The family spent the summer at Walton-on-Thames. A second volume records their extended stay in Oporto. Birmingham UL On 'Women's Language & Experience' mf 2 (Adam Matthew)

325. *1845* STUART, *Lady* Louisa, daughter of 3rd Earl of Bute, aunt of Lady Anna Maria Dawson (**358**). Diary, 1845, 1849. Her London activities in her eighties. Bodleian MS Eng. misc. g.169–70

326. *1846* COATES, Eliza, of Monmouth. Diary of a visit to London in 1846, with description of sights including the Royal Exchange and the British Museum, shopping and theatre. Glos RO D 3180/1

327. *1846* EDWARDS, Samuel, of Champion Hill, Camberwell. Honeymoon diary, 1854, starting with his marriage at St Matthew's, Brixton. Southwark LSL A137

328. *1846* GRIMSTON, James Walter, *2nd Earl of Verulam*, of Gorhambury, Herts. Diary, 1846–95. Herts ALS D/EV F102–151

329. *1846* KING, Elizabeth Anne, of Madingley, Cambs. Diary, 1846, 1849–1924. Brief daily entries on events and activities, including spells in London. Cambridge CRO 588/F49

330. *1846* STEPHEN, *the Rt Hon Sir* James, statesman. Diary, Jan–July 1846, on personal life, political affairs, the Colonial Office. Written at Downing Street. CUL Add MSS 7511

331. *1846* TWIGGS, John D, of the United States, traveller. Diary of a trip to London, including sights, 1846. N Carolina UL

332. *1847* CLARK, *Sir* James, Medical practitioner, physician to the royal family. Diary of two tours, 1847 and 1858, with the royal family. R Coll Physicians

333. *1847* ENDICOTT, George, of the United States, traveller. Diary of a European tour, Aug–Nov 1847, including a stay in London. Typical sightseeing, including theatre visits, St Paul's cathedral, Bank of England. New York PL

334. *1847* FARROW, George, of Rainham, Essex, shoemaker. Diary, 1847–94, including details of local events, church activities and sale of celery plants. Essex RO D/DU 1488

335. *1847* GRENVILLE, Richard, *3rd Duke of Buckingham and Chandos*, politian, earlier a Member of Parliament. Diary, 1847–8, 1868. He succeeded to the Dukedom in 1861. Huntington L Stowe Colln

336. *1847* HUMPHREYS, Elizabeth, of London, wife of barrister. Diary, Jan–March 1847 (?) of domestic life, including secretarial work for husband, and dental problems. Nat L Wales Glansevern 14, 743

337. *1847* SALVIN, Eliza Anne, of Finchley, daughter of architect Anthony Salvin. Diary, 1847, 1849–51, 1856–9. Family life, theatre and operagoing, visits to British Museum. Cultured circle of friends. Barnet ALS MS 6787

338. *1848* CARTER, Henry Vandyke, of St George's Hospital, medical student, Demonstrator in Anatomy, later Deputy Surgeon General, Indian Medical Service. Diary, 1848–52, 1853–8, including his time as a London medical student, anatomy demonstrator and medical illustrator. Entries deal with his studies, work and private life, self-reproach about laziness and religious failings. Some of the period covers his studies in Paris and his early days in India. Wellcome MSS 5816, 5818

339. *1848* EATON, George C. Diary of travels, including London, 1848, 1872, 1886, 1895. Norfolk RO Eaton 4.2.71 III

340. *1848* LAYTON, Thomas, of Brentford, member of Brentford Union Board of Guardians. Personal diary, April 1848–July 1849, kept while serving on the Board as representative of the parish of Ealing and Old Brentford. Hounslow LSL Layton Colln MS. 17682

341. *1849* CARRINGTON, *Lady* Charlotte Augusta, of Buckinghamshire. Diary, 1849–56, with memoranda on London society engagements. Bucks RO Carrington Colln

342. *1849* FOUNTAIN, Rebecca, of Ealing, wife of Abraham Fountain, Welsh linen draper. Diary, 1849–50. The Fountains were on the chapel committee of Ealing Congregational Church. Ealing LHL

343. *1849* HOOPER, Ellen, of Bath Place, Queen's Road, Peckham. Diary, 1849–50. Southwark LSL A 129

four antique legs – thus it combines
the advantages of a box & a table

May –

Dress rehearsal of Henry V at the Princesses
A very curious sight. The theatre is lighted
but not so fully as during a representation
Kean sat in the centre of the Dress circle
The actors hurried through their parts for it
was not so much a rehearsal for the acting
as for the scenery – Actors appear in the
boxes every now & then to get a view of what
they will never see again
Baskets full of various apparel are brought on
the stage. Soldiers are seen fitting on their
helmets, choosing their lances etc –
If men put themselves into bad positions
Kean calls out. He addresses all the women
as "my dear" – Mrs Kean hastens from
place to place to judge of the effect on
all sides – now she is in the Queen's
box, now in the dress circle

4. Eliza Salvin (**337**) attends a dress rehearsal in 1859 *(courtesy of Barnet Archives and Local Studies)*

344. *1849* PARKINSON-FORTESCUE, Frances Elizabeth Anne, *7th Countess Waldegrave*. Diary, 1849–79. Social round, visits, dinner parties, life at Strawberry Hill. Entries for the last few months of her life, in 1879, annotated by her widower. BL Add MSS 63,705–27

345. *1849* POWELL, Ophelia Catherine, of Colyton, Devon, daughter of RN officer, later wife of Unitarian minister. Diary, 1849–52, 1852–64, including visits to London, where she comments on church services, and admires the Great Exhibition. Nat L Wales George Eyre Evans MSS no.13–15

346. *1849* SHERIDAN, Richard Brinsley, of Frampton Court, Dorset, Member of Parliament. Diary, 1849–75, including life and parliamentary business in London, art and artists. Dorset RO MSS D51/15/1–11

347. *1850* ANON, of the United States, clergyman. Diary of trip to attend the London Missionary Society Convention in London, 1850. Billy Graham Center SCO96–A

348. *1850* ANON, (female) of Ireland. Diary, 1850, of Irishwoman's visit to London. PRONI D 906/365/1

349. *1850* ALLEN, Ebenezer Brown, clergyman, chaplain to the Consumption Hospital, Chelsea. Diary, 1828–80. He moved to London in 1850, living in Chelsea and Kensington. York City Archives ACC 100

350. *1850* BENTLEY, George, publisher and author, son of Richard Bentley (**404**). Diary and correspondence, 1850–95. Available on British Publishers' Archives on Microfilm (Chadwyck Healey, 1976). Illinois UL

351. *1850* BLAND, William, of Hartlip, Kent. Diary of travels including London, *c*. 1850. Kentish Studies U771 F11

352. *1850* HERVEY, Isabella Mary, daughter of Lionel Charles Hervey, wife of Walter Drummond of Sevenoaks and Park Street, London. Diary, 1850–7, of daily activities, dinners, visits, friends. Birmingham UL MSS 7/iii/6

353. *1850* PEGLER, George, of Earith, Hunts, and Willingham, Cambs, Headmaster of British School. Diary of daily life as teacher, health, religious meetings, science lectures, reading and visits, including frequent trips to London where members of his family lived, 1850–60. Extracts in *Victorian Diaries* (ed H Creaton, 2001). Cambridge CRO 854/F1

354. *1851* BELL, W J, of Newcastle, businessman. Elaborate diary and scrapbook recording a visit to London for the Great Exhibition in 1851. Detailed account of indefatigable sightseeing, including refreshment stops and transport arrangements. Ephemera stuck into the volume add to its charm. MoL L 10.1

355. *1851* BOWDITCH, Stephen Hugh, of Lewisham Park. Copy of his diary, 1851–70, 1879–85. Domestic life, medical history of his many children, rather 'Pooterish'. Lewisham LSC PT78/200/1 (GFC)

356. *1851* CHAPMAN, John, critic and editor. Diary, 1851 and 1860, about his social life, work on the Westminster Review while George Eliot was living in his house, business life and health. Yale UL MSS Vault section 4 drawer 3

357. *1851* DALY, Charles Patrick, of New York City, judge. Diary of American's tour and social life in London, 1851. British Museum, Tower of London, Crystal Palace, National Gallery, other tourist sights as well as opera and theatre, but also Judge and Jury Society, Seven Dials and the rookeries. New York PL

358. *1851* DAWSON, *Lady* Anna Maria, Lady in waiting to the Duchess of Kent, niece of Lady Louisa Stuart (**325**) Diary, 1851. Bodleian MS Eng. misc. g.173

359. *1851* HUTCHINSON, Peter Orlando, of Sidmouth, Devon, botanist and antiquary. Diary of visit to London, including Great Exhibition, 1851. Extract in *The Observant Traveller* (ed R Gard 1989). Devon RO MS 36

360. *1851* JOHNSON, Nancy Maria Donaldson. Diary of trip to Europe with her husband, Walter Rogers Johnson, who was commissioner to the Great Exhibition. Crystal Palace, sights. L Congress Peter Force Papers 8D 78, also mf 17,137 reel 43

361. *1851* JUPP, George, agricultural labourer and New Zealand colonist. Copy of diary, 1851, covers visit to Great Exhibition before leaving for New Zealand. Rhodes HL 850.12.S.4

362. *1851* MORAN, Benjamin, of the United States, diplomat. Diary, 1851, 1857–75, kept while secretary to the American Legation in London. L Congress MSS 0447H

363. *1852* ANON, wife of a farmer near Uxbridge, Middx. Diary, Jan–Dec 1852, farm and family business. Wigan AS EHC138/M923

364. *1852* CROKER, Thomas Crofton, of Fulham, Irish antiquary. Diary, 1852. S Antiq MS 751

365. *1852* GREATOREX, Dan, of Whitechapel, later Vicar of St Paul's, Dock Street. Diary, 1852–4, 1855–7, 1860–2. He was working or studying out of London until 1860, but frequently visited his parents in the city. Saw funeral of Duke of Wellington, worked at the Royal Panopticon, visited Zoo, Crystal Palace, Lock Chapel, shopping, health problems. Based in London from 1860, working for Thames Church Mission on board their ship the Swan. Visits to shipping, dockyards. Newgate prison, Old Bailey trial, Bethlehem Hospital, British Museum. Burial of Prince Consort. International Exhibition. Later volumes cover his extensive foreign travels. Tower Hamlets LHLA P/GTX/1–3

366. *1852* HEFFER, Edward Arthur, of London, possibly Kentish Town, apprentice architect. Diary, 1852, about his education, personal life, love affair, 'self-help', visit to Crystal Palace. Wigan AS EHC62/M831

367. *1852* JARVIS, G K, of Doddington, Lincs. Travel diary, including a stay in London, 1852. Lincs Archives 8/43

368. *1852* TAYLOR, Shephard Thomas, of Norwich, medical practitioner (physician). Diary, 1852–6, a mixture of social life and work in London. His later diaries (1858–64) were published as the *Diary of a Medical Student, 1860–4* (1927) and *Diary of a Norwich Hospital Medical Student, 1858–60* (1930). R Coll Physicians MSS 2435–9

369. *1853* BULLER, James Wentworth, Member of Parliament, Chairman of Bristol and Exeter Railway. Diary of travel, including London, 1853. Devon RO 1065M/F9/41

370. *1853* JONES, Arthur F, of Brixton, Camberwell and Cranleigh, accountant or clerk. Diary, 1853–9, 1868–1910. Social life, domestic affairs, work in the City. Lambeth AD 8/25 (S1654)

371. *1853* LUBBOCK, *Sir* John, *Bart, 1st Baron Avebury*, banker, scientist and author, husband of Alice Lubbock (**503**). Diary, Jan 1853–May 1913. Work, family life, travels. His courtship and second marriage in 1884. BL Add MSS 62,679–84

372. *1853* MIERS, *Mrs* S M, of Rio de Janeiro, wife of shipbuilder. Diary, covering visit to London in 1853, seeing British Museum, Crystal Palace, Drury Lane theatre, and attending a Dickens reading. Wigan AS EHC27/M795

373. *1853* WYON, Leonard Charles, of the Royal Mint, chief engraver. Diary, 1853–67, which he resolved to keep from Aug 1853. Home life, his happy marriage (to 'dear May'), arrival of children, early death of some of them, problems of finding wet nurses and other servants. His work at the Mint, engraving, modelling. Extracts in *Victorian Diaries* (ed H Creaton, 2001). BL Add MSS 59,617

374. *1854* ANON, of London. Diary, 1854, of social events, family matters, church attendance. Reading UL MS 1195

375 *1855* ANON, (male) of London, banker. Extracts from a private diary with correspondence concerning the formation of the Ottoman Bank. Guildhall L MS 4238

376. *1855* BICKERSTETH, Charlotte, author, sister of Harriet Cook (**314**). Diary of her life in London, 1855–63. Wellcome PP/COO/11–5

377. *1855* BRODRICK, Augusta Mary, *Viscountess Midleton*, wife of William Brodrick, 8th Viscount Midleton. Diary, 1855–98, covering social life in London as well as life on the family estate at Peper Harow, Surrey. 1855 diary mentions her charitable work at a London Ragged School. Activities and health of her large family (nine children). Surrey HC 1538/1–44

378. *1855* GRIFFITH, William Tyndal, of Bangor, medical student. Diary, 1855–61, covering work at Bloomsbury Dispensary, Royal London Orthopaedic Hospital and St Luke's Hospital for Lunatics, also public events, and his social and religious life. Some shorthand passages. Nat L Wales MSS 10209A 10210B 10211B

379. *1855* GROOM, Emma, of Finsbury and Islington, book restorer. Diary, 1855–1900, some retrospective. Illness and death of family and friends, religious sentiments, seaside holidays. MoL

380. *1855* RICHARDSON, Sarah, of Newcastle. Travel diary of continental tour, 1855, including brief but energetic sightseeing in London en route. Cambridge CRO R 83/061

381. *1855* VAN BUREN, Angelica Singleton, of South Carolina, daughter-in-law of US President Martin Van Buren. Diary of visit to Europe, including London, with her family, 1855. S Carolina UL

382. *1856* CUST (née HOBART), Maria Adelaide, wife of Robert Needham Cust, *qv*. Diary, 1856–60, of courtship, marriage, shopping and general daily life in England and departure to India in 1859. Full description of her wedding day, and the birth of her daughter. Extracts in *Victorian Diaries* (ed H Creaton, 2001). BLOIO MSS.EUR. A118

383. *1856* HALLIDAY, Jane Meliora, of Belmont Park, Lee (from 1865), wife of John Halliday, pre-Raphaelite painter. Diary, 1856–1913, brief entries relating to her social engagements and the weather; with cash accounts. Lewisham LSC A90/7/1–55

384. *1857* BOLTON, John, of Hoxton. Diary, 1857, of domestic and religious matters. Hackney AD Z21

385. *1857* BOSANQUET, Augustus Henry, of East Barnet. Diary, personal and business matters, 1857–76. Herts ALS D/EX 176 F1

386. *1857* FANE, (née COWPER), *Lady* Adine, daughter of 6th Earl Cowper, wife of the Hon Henry Fane. Diary, 1857–61, 1866, 1868, from age of fourteen, of life in the country and London, including her dislike of the social season. Herts ALS D/EP F644; D/ERv F4–F5

387. *1857* GRENVILLE (née HARVEY), Caroline, *Duchess of Buckingham and Chandos*, wife of 3rd Duke. Diary, 1857. Huntington L Stowe Colln

388. *1857* LEE, Robert James, of Great Ormond Street Hospital, medical practitioner (physician). Diary 10 Oct 1857–20 Sept 1869; 8 Nov 1902–7 March 1903; 13 Nov 1910–7 Feb 1911, with reminiscences about his early life, and his father. Personal matters, medical duties, and descriptions of public events such as the Reform Bill demonstrations of 1867. Wellcome MSS 3221, 3224

389. *1857* MORLAND, Edward Henry, of the Bengal Civil Service. Diary, 1857, starting in India, the voyage home and retirement in Berkshire with frequent visits to London. BLOIO MSS.EUR. A188

390. *1857* TOD, John, of Edinburgh, engineer. Diary of visit to London, June–July 1857. Nat L Scotland Acc 9211

391. *1857* WEST, Henry, King's College, London, engineering student. Diary for 1857, covering his scientific work, social life, visits and entertainments. LMA F/WST/19

392. *1858* BARNARD, Elizabeth Mary, of Cheshire. Diary of travel, including London, 1858. Cheshire RO DDX 459

393. *1858* COMPTON, Louisa. Diary of voyage from Bombay to England, 1858, then London life and a Scottish visit. BLOIO MSS.EUR. A39

394. *1858* DRAKE, Samuel Gardner, of New Hampshire. Diary kept 1858–9 while researching American history in London: offices visited, people, London life and places. New Hampshire HS C438

395. *1858* FLOWER (née ROTHSCHILD), Constance, *Lady Battersea*, Diary of her family and social life starting as a teenager, 27 June 1858–Nov 1928. Often in London and at Rothschild houses nearby, such as Gunnersbury, visiting relations. BL Add MSS 47,913–47

396. *1858* FORDE, Henry Charles, of Wimbledon, civil engineer. Diaries, 1858–82, 1889, 1890, 1896, a mixture of business activities (cable-laying, telegraphs, railways), Volunteer service, church attendance, theatre-going, family events. Wimbledon M A17

397. *1858* HARLEY, John Pritt, of Upper Gower Street, and the Princess's Theatre, Oxford Street, actor. Diary, 1 Jan–20 Aug 1858, the last few months of his life. Daily events, with great attention to meals. Plays rehearsed, roles played, theatrical and family gossip. Extracts in *Victorian Diaries* (ed H Creaton, 2001). LMA O/54/1

398. *1858* LLOYD, James, of 5 Kingsland Green, Hackney. Diary, 1858–62, dealing with his family life, religious activity (St Matthias and Balls Pond churches), charitable dispensations. Notes household expenditure. Hackney AD M4409

399. *1858* PATTERSON, James, of Manchester, teacher of deaf and dumb. Diary, with account of visit to London 1858–9. Tourist sights, mesmeric experiments. Wellcome MSS 7353

400. *1858* ROBERTS, Nathaniel, of Combe Farm, East Greenwich, market gardener. Diary, 1858, recording his family's activities, including having photographs taken. The photographs survive with the collection. Greenwich LHL Combe Farm Colln

401. *1858* SHERRARD (née HALL), Louisa, of West Wickham, Kent, sister of Emily and Ellen Hall (**290**). Diary, 1858–97 about family matters and social activities. She was frequently abroad in Switzerland and Germany. Bromley AS U923/F1–19

402. *1858* SILVER, Henry, of *Punch*, journalist. Diary, 4 Aug 1858–23 March 1870, of his daily life and literary gossip. Edition in preparation by Prof. P. Leary of Indiana University. Punch L PUN/A/Silv

403. *1859* ANON, a member of the SLADDEN family, of Seward House, Badsey, Worcs. Diary of journey starting from London to Leith by steamer, 1859, and on into Scotland. Worcs RO 705:1037

404. *1859* BENTLEY, Richard, publisher, father of George Bentley (**350**). Diary, 1859–70. Available on British Publishers' Archives on Microfilm (Chadwyck-Healey, 1976). Illinois UL

405. *1859* CREPIGNY, Frances, later *Lady* REYNOLDS. Diary, 1859–64, including London activities, visits to British Museum, National Gallery, Royal Academy, Crystal Palace, concerts, the opera, flower exhibitions and dog shows. Herts ALS 86135

406. *1859* HORROCKS, John, of Lambeth and Wandsworth, schoolmaster. Diary with spasmodic entries, 1859, of his life teaching at a Methodist school which he eventually left to become a shopkeeper. Wigan AS EHC56/M825

407. *1859* LEYCESTER, Rafe Neville, schoolboy, later Inland Revenue clerk. Diary, 1859–65 (with gap Feb 1861–Aug 1863) of everyday life as schoolboy in London and Devon, and his first job in the Civil Service. Rowing on the Thames, walking, interest in young female acquaintances, and in politics. Private. Mr E. Fenton (ef@day-books.com)

408. *1860* JANSEN, Victorine, of Redditch, Worcs. Diary, 1860–62, with theatrical interest. Worcs RO BA 11402

409. *1860* MAGNIAC, Hollingworth, father-in-law of Augusta Magniac. Diary, 1860. Brief but regular pencilled entries about daily life, his health and that of family. He lived in Bedfordshire but made frequent trips to the City. BLOIO MSS.EUR. F197/620

410. *1861* BUND, Harriette Penelope Willis, of London and Worcestershire. Diary and papers, 1861–81. Worcs RO 705.36, BA533

411. *1861* GULLETT, Henry, of Melbourne, journalist. The London section of his diary covers Oct 1861–Nov 1862, after which he returned to his work in Australia, continuing the diary until 1866. State L NSW MS 1473

412. *1861* MILLER, Frederick, clergyman. Diary, 1861–2, of voyage from Melbourne to London and back, during which he acted as chaplain on board. He records his stay in London in between. Nat Maritime M MS NOR (113045)

413. *1861* MILLER, Thomas, writer of books for boys. Diary, Jan–Sept 1861. Brief daily entries about family activities, gardening and the progress of his writing work, but also his jaunts into the City. Wigan AS D/DZ EHC84/M853

414. *1861* ROPE, Elizabeth H, of London, and Fressingfield, Suffolk. Diary, 1861–71, of life in country and frequent visits to London. Visits the International Exhibition in 1862, the Albert Hall soon after its opening in 1871. Available on Women's Language and Experience mf pt. 3 (Adam Matthew, 1999). Suffolk RO (Ipswich) HD 289/5–9

415. *1861* VINCENT, John Amyatt Chaundy, of London, architect and genealogist. Diary, 1 Jan 1861–31 Dec 1863, 1 Jan 1867–5 Jan 1871. With personal entries, including problems of lodging in London, among heraldic, genealogical and antiquarian matters. Wigan AS EHC120/M888; 121/M889

416. *1862* ANON, Diary, 1862, including visit to International Exhibition in London. Devon RO MSS 337 B add/235/3

417. *1862* ANON, a member of the PROBY family, of Colyton, Devon. Diary of visit to London including the 1862 Exhibition. Devon RO 337add B/MF83/3

418. *1862* ANON, of Tooting. Diary, 1862–77, relating to philanthropic work, including at Brompton Hospital and a soup kitchen, attending evening classes, church, theatregoing and holidays on the South Coast. Surrey HC 4351

419. *1862* CHAPLIN, Samuel, of Lexden, Colchester, owner of seed crushing mill. Diary, 1862–87. Although he lived in Essex, Chaplin visited London at least weekly on business, by train, and in 1885 moved there. Business items mixed with personal material about visits to relations, to the theatre, dining out and shopping. MoL Diaries D3

420. *1862* DENSLOW, Dwight B, and Loise A, of the United States, travellers. Diary of travels in Europe and Middle East, 1861–2, including a visit to London on the way home. Sightseeing, including the International Exhibition. New York PL

421. *1862* EGERTON, Elizabeth, *Countess of Wilton.* Diary, 1861–1919. Bodleian MS Eng. misc. f.421–72

422. *1862* FELL, Alfred, of London, and Nelson, NZ, businessman. Diary, 1862, recording a voyage back to England and life in London in his return. Nelson Provincial M Bett Colln

423. *1862* FLEMING, Albert, of Champion Hill, Camberwell. Diary, 1862, when aged sixteen. Southwark LSL A418

424. *1862* LEGGATT, Frederica Constance, of Lowndes Square, Knightsbridge, medical practitioner's daughter. Diary, 1862–4, of daily life, including visit to International Exhibition in 1862, nursing relatives, visiting sick, teaching poor children. Wigan AS D/DX EHC176/M968

425. *1862* MAGNIAC, Augusta, probably daughter-in-law of Hollingworth Magniac, *qv.* Diary, 1862, of daily life near London, mentioning visits in Hendon and husband's work in the City. BLOIO MSS.EUR. F197/625

426. *1862* WEBB, Benjamin, clergyman, ecclesiologist, prebendary of St Paul's cathedral. Diary, 1837–85, Had London parish from 1862. Bodleian MS Eng. misc. e.406–41; f.97–9

427. *1863* ANON, (male) of Wimbledon, builder. Diary, 1863, of personal life and work in the family building firm at a time of great suburban expansion. Wimbledon M

428. *1863* EDWARDS, F Y, of Cromwell House, 42 Hampstead Hill Gardens, Army officer. Edwards travelled widely and most of his diary relates to visits abroad. He remained in London for the first half of 1863 and wrote detailed accounts of his activities, which include seeing the opening of the Metropolitan Railway in Jan and the celebrations for the arrival of Princess Alexandra to marry the Prince of Wales in March. MoL 76.15/11

429. *1863* MARTINEAU, *Miss* F J, Diary, 1863–73. Bodleian MS Eng. misc. f.499, g.102–7; g.102–5

430. *1864* BARROW, John, of Kingham, Oxon, retired Army officer (Lieutenant-Colonel). Diary, Aug 1864–Nov 1894: social life, including occasional visits to London. Bodleian MS Eng. Hist. d.18–81

431. *1864* BROOKS, Charles William Shirley, journalist, editor of *Punch.* Shirley Brooks's diary, covering his family and social life as well as his work on *Punch*, is in three separate repositories: Harvard UL (1864); Punch L (1867, 1872); and the London L (1869, 1871, 1873). Harvard UL Eng MSS 601.20; Punch L PUN/A/Brok/AA 1–2; London L Safe 4

432. *1864* HOWELL, George, trade unionist, Member of Parliament, writer. Diary, 1864–1908. Bishopsgate I George Howell Colln

433. *1864* PALMER, James, head coachman to the Earl of Strafford. Diary, 1864–83, including journeys made during the London season of 1866. Herts ALS D/EX 318 Z1–2

434. *1864* POORE, Robert, of Old Lodge, Lower Wallop, Hants, retired Army officer (Major). Diary, 1864–1918, including his visits to London and his enthusiastic Directorship of the London and Provincial Turkish Baths Co. The company ran the luxurious Hamman Turkish Baths in Jermyn Street. There are earlier diaries in the series (1853–63) relating to his Indian service. Wilts RO 1915/65–172

435. *1864* THORNHILL, later DOWNE, Henriette, of South Lambeth and Essex/Suffolk. Diary, 1864–79, starting at age seventeen. The granddaughter of Sarah Siddons, orphaned when her parents were killed in the Indian Mutiny. Brought up by grandmother, much on South Lambeth social life. Lambeth AD K 63616

436. *1865* COKAYNE, George ('GEC'), of Ashbourne House, Putney High Street, and Exeter House, Putney Heath, barrister, herald and genealogist, husband of Mary Dorothea Cokayne, father of Brien Cokayne, *qqv*. Diary, 1865–1910, of his social and professional life. With ephemera. Northants RO C 1334, 1462

437. *1865* RODWELL, J M, Rector of St Ethelburga, Bishopsgate. Diary of personal and parish affairs, 1865. Written in volume of parish register for baptisms and burials, 1792–1818. Also contains his autobiography to 1864. Guildhall L MS 4238 (on mf).

438. *1866* DANIEL, Wilson Eustace, clergyman. Diary, 1866–1923 (with gaps), the earlier years dealing with his time as assistant curate of St Mark's, Whitechapel, and an outbreak of cholera. Brief entries. Bath CL MSS 1150–1201

439. *1866* MAYNARD, Constance Louisa, Principal of Westfield College, University of London. Personal diary, 1866–86, 1901–35, covering most of her working life. Other diaries concern college matters only. QMW WFD/ CLM

440. *1867* CUST, Robert Needham, orientalist, Secretary of Royal Asiatic Society, widower of Maria Adelaide Cust *qv*. Diary, 10 Aug 1867 – Feb 1909 covers his retirement in London after career in India. Basic index in each volume, Much on his scholarly activities including Needham genealogy, but also family worries, such as his son's unhappiness at at Eton. BL Add MSS 45,397–406

441. *1868* BLAKE, Walter Scott, law student. Diary, 1868–70. Lived in Gower Street, later in Oxford Terrace, and worked in Chancery Lane. IOW CRO BRS/B/125

442. *1868* DOBELL, Bertram, of Haverstock Hill, and Charing Cross Road, bookseller, man of letters, husband of Eleanor Dobell, *qv*. Diary, 1868–9, 1881–1914. Bodleian MS Dobell e.1–34, f.2–3

443. *1868* GLADSTONE, Henry Neville, of Hawarden Castle, Flints., son of Catherine Gladstone (**218**). Diary, 1868, 1869–70, 1873–5, 1875–8, 1903, 1922, 1924, 1931. St Deiniol's L MS 1824–31

444. *1868* PAINE, Mary Maria, of Farquhar Road, Upper Norwood. Diary (copies), 1868–9, 1876. Domestic and social life, frequent visits to the Crystal Palace. Lewisham LSC PT83/7635(GFC)

445. *1868* REYNOLDS, W, (male) of Nottingham. Diary noting a visit to London in Feb 1868. Notts Archives MS M 12,297

446. *1868* SMILEY, Sarah F, of Pennsylvania, traveller. Diary of trip to England, 1868–9, philanthropic and religious interests, visits. Pennsylvania HS 602

447. *1868* WILDE, James, Post Office employee and amateur organist. Diary, Jan–May 1868. Played the organ in some City churches. Hackney AD M4545

448. *1870* LIDDON, Henry Parry, clergyman, canon of St Paul's cathedral. Diary, 1858–90, of his life in Oxford and, from 1870, in London. Bodleian MS St Edmund Hall MS 69

449. *1869* BARING (née DIGBY) *Lady* Leonora Caroline, wife of 4th Baron Ashburton. Diary, 1869–70. Barings 136

450. *1871* ANON, possibly BROWN, Henry Francis, of London. Diary, 19 Aug 1871–17 July 1874, with some material on home life, but also much continental travel. Wigan AS EHC107/M875

451. *1871* BUCHANAN (née FORBES-ROBERTSON), Ida Mary, sister of the actor Sir Johnston Forbes-Robertson. Diary, 1871–1921, though some early material has been excised, and biographical notes added later. Theatrical matters. An account of the arrest and imprisonment in Holloway of a suffragette who broke Gamage's windows in 1913. BL Add MSS 62,699

452. *1871* STANSFIELD, T W, Indian Army officer (Major). Diary, 1871–8, of life in India and London. Birmingham UL MS 6/vi/14

453. *1871* WEBB, Mildred H, daughter of Benjamin Webb, *qv*. Diary, 18 Oct 1871–18 June 1874. Bodleian MS Eng. misc. d.478, e.444–7

454. *1872* CHAMBERS, Marian, of Crouch Hill, Hornsey, wife of architect. Diary, 1872, of domestic and social family life in North London. Haringey BC 790 CHA

455. *1872* CROSWELL, Henry. Diary, 1872–86, recording Sunday visits to London churches, with notes on architecture, clergy, style and length of service, music and congregation. Bodleian MS Eng. misc. c.402/1–2 (transcript)

456. *1872* DONALDSON, Andrew Brown, and DONALDSON, Agnes Emily (née TWINING) of Kensington. Joint diary, 1872–1919, kept throughout their married life, usually taking turns to write each day's events. Middle class family life, health, domestic matters, social engagements, Andrew's work as an artist. Occasional marginal sketches. Extract in Victorian Diaries (ed H Creaton 2001), relating to a winter spent in Rome in 1880–1. LMA F/DON/1–27

457. *1873* BENTLEY, Richard, the younger, publisher and meteorologist. Diary, 1873–4. Bodleian MS Eng. misc. e.733

458. *1873* HOOD (née TIBBITS), Mary, *Viscountess Hood,* of Barton Seagrove, Northants. Diary, 1873–1900. Northants RO WR 727, 751–5

459. *1873* KNATCHBULL-HUGESSEN, Eva, daughter of 1st Baron Brabourne. Personal diary, with illustrations, 1873–93 (with gaps), including overseas visits. Kentish Studies F30/1–9

460. *1873* PAUL (née RITCHIE), Elinor. Diary, 1873, 1876, 1878–83, 1887–1920. Herts ALS D/EAm F1–42

461. *1873* POWELL, H J, of Dulwich, of Whitefriars Glass. Alphabetical notebook with chronological index forming rough diary. Technical glass-making data interspersed with personal items, his marriage, family events, a few notes on his time as Conservative member for Dulwich on the LCC. MoL Whitefriars Glass Archive 3238 Box 15

462. *1873* RAMSAY, Charles Maule, schoolboy, later cadet. Diary, 1873–7, kept at Wimbledon School and then at the Royal Military Academy, Woolwich. NAS GD 45/26/93

463. *1873* RASHDALL, Hastings, schoolboy. Diary, 1873, kept at Harrow School. Bodleian MS Eng. misc. e.361

464. *1873* THRUSTON, Rogers C B, of the United States, traveller. Diary of European tour, including London, 1873. Filson HS

465. *1874* BODLEY, John Edward Courtney, historian and politician. Diary, 1874–5, 1884–5, social life, political gossip, theatre visits, life in Oxford and London. Bodleian MS Eng. misc. e 459–61, d 498, and Balliol Coll Lib MS 443

466. *1874* CHADNEY, R J, of 37 Jackson Road, Holloway, school attendance inspector. Diary, Oct 1874–Sept 1875, of his daily life, and work enforcing school attendance. Islington LHC YA162

467. *1874* LYTTELTON, *Sir* Neville Gerald, Army officer (General). Diary, 1874–1929. Bodleian MS MSS Eng hist e 379, f 35–82

468. *1874* MORGAN-GRENVILLE, Mary, *Baroness Kinloss*, daughter of 3rd Duke of Buckingham and Chandos. Diary, 1874. Huntington L Stowe Colln

469. *1874* WELD, Constance Elizabeth, of Lulworth Castle, Dorset, daughter of Edward Joseph Weld. Diary, 1874 and 1876. Daily activity of a young lady, including spells in London. Dorset RO MSS D10/F109

470. *1875* COURTNEY, Catherine, *Lady Courtney*, of Cheyne Walk, Chelsea, wife of 1st Baron Courtney, politician and economist, sister of Rosalind Dobbs, *qv*. Diary, 1875–1919. LSE Courtney Colln XXI–XXXVIII

471. *1875* STAREY, Emily, of Highgate. Diary of visits to Streatham, 1875, 1878. Beds RO SY 235

472. *1877* ANON, of Bath. Diary of daily life of a young woman living near Bath, who visited London 1877. Birmingham UL MS 6/i/35

473. *1877* COOK, Alfred Marshall, of St Paul's School, schoolmaster. Diary, 1877–86, 1912–21. Political events, literary interests, theatre, social engagements. Bodleian MS Eng. misc. e.166–77

474. *1878* SIMPSON, *Mrs* L M, widow. Diary, 1 July 1878–18 July 1880. Mrs Simpson visited relations in turn, one of her regular stopping points being London. Wigan AS EHC53/M822

475. *1879* ANON, of London and Sussex. Diary, 1879–81. Oxfordshire Archives OA/E/7/J3/01–2

476. *1879* BLATHWAYT, *Mrs* W T, of Dyrham, Glos, wife of clergyman. Diary, 1879–81, mainly concerning her ill-health, involving many visits to London doctors. Glos RO D1799/F260

477. *1879* HOON, Reinetta, of Leytonstone. Diary, 1879, covering family events and visits, opera visits, lectures, skating, swimming and other leisure activities. Waltham Forest ALSL L 96 Hoon 1

478. *1879* JONES, David, of Wallington, Surrey. Diary, 1879–83, 1887. Local life, antiquarian interests, description of Fr Ignatius, the weather. Cardiff CL MSS 1.640

479. *1879* MONTEFIORE, *Sir* Moses Haim, philanthropist. Diary, 1879. UC London MSS Room

480. *1879* STANTON, Robert L, of the United States, clergyman. Diary of a visit to London, Feb–March 1879. Sightseeing, visits, preachers heard. New York PL

481. *1880* ANDERSON, W, of the United States, traveller. Diary of a voyage round the world, 1879–80, on the barque *Sara S Ridgway*. The entries for June–July 1880 describe his stay in London, seeing the sights including the opening of the Albert Docks. Australian NL MS 665

482. *1880* BOWKER, Richard Rogers, American publisher's agent. Diary, 1880–1, of his activities in London as agent for Harper & Bros, dealings with authors, London social life, operas, concerts, Library Association meetings. New York PL

483. *1880* DILKE, *Sir* Charles Wentworth, *Bart*, politician and author. Diary, 1880–3. Birmingham UL Special Collns

484. *1880* MELLICK, Andrew D, of the United States, traveller. Diary of trip to Europe, 1880, including England. Typescript. Rutgers UL

485. *1880* ROGERS (née SKINNER), Alice, of Croydon. Diary, 1880–1905, covering her marriage, birth of daughter, the Diamond Jubilee celebrations, her treatment for consumption, peace celebrations after Boer War. Croydon LSL AR57/1/1

486. *1880* SALLUTIO, *Mrs* Henry, of the United States, traveller. Diary of tour of England and Italy, 1880. Brown U John Hay L 92/A69

487. *1880* TREE, *Sir* Herbert Beerbohm, actor manager, husband of Maud, Lady Tree, *qv*. Diary 1880, 1890, 1893–5, 1897, 1909, 1914–17, covering his theatrical activities and social life, with notes on production ideas and plans. Bristol U Theatre Colln HBT Diaries

488. *1881* CAMPBELL-BANNERMAN, Sarah Charlotte, *Lady Campbell-Bannerman*, wife of politician and, later, Prime Minister. Diary 1881–3, 1884–7, noting guests at dinner, visitors, social activities, occasional political comments. Entries usually brief. BL Add MSS 41,251

489. *1881* EVANS, William Burges, of Mehetabel Road, Homerton, cashier in solicitor's firm. Diary, 1881–4, 1889–1900. Evans began the diary as a schoolboy. It covers home life, holidays, finding a job, Sunday School teaching. Hackney AD D/F/EVA

490. *1881* FITCH, Edward Arthur, antiquary. Diary of life on a Thames tug, 1881. Essex RO D/DQs 146/2

491. *1881* HALL, William John, canon of St Paul's cathedral, clergyman. Diary, 1881–1909, with retrospective notes of his earlier life, written 'for the benefit or amusement of my children'. Covers his family life, troublesome half-brothers, anorexic daughter, and his professional activities. St Paul's Cathedral L

492. *1881* MILNER, Alfred, *Viscount Milner*, statesman. Diary, 1881–1925, of his social and political activities. Bodleian MS Milner 56–96

493. *1881* SAMBOURNE, Marion Herapath, of Kensington, wife of *Punch* artist Edwin Linley Sambourne. Diary, 1881–1914 including details of illnesses, operations and medical treatment of herself and her family, and family menus. Linley Sambourne H

494. *1882* CROCKER, William, of Bow, solicitor's clerk. Photocopied extract from diary for 13 Sept 1882, describing family outing by train to Chingford via Leytonstone, and walk in Epping Forest. Waltham Forest ALSL Acc 10270

495. *1882* RAMSAY, Robert William. Ramsay's diary runs from 1869–1951, beginning when he was eight. London coverage from 1882. An active cultural and social life. Concerts, plays, national events, antiquarian pursuits. Many ephemera (tickets, programmes, etc) with the diary. LMA F/RMY/1–44

496. *1882* ROGERS, Clement F, theologian, son of J E Thorold Rogers, and Ann SC Rogers (**288**). Diary, 1882, 1884–6. Bodleian MS Eng. misc. f.495–8

497. *1882* TREE, Maud, *Lady Tree*, actress, wife of Sir Herbert Beerbohm Tree, *qv*. Diary, 1882, 1885, 1887, 1889–96, about her social life and theatrical engagements. Bristol U Theatre Colln HBT Diaries

498. *1883* HODDINOTT, Joseph Fletcher, of London, London & County Bank manager. Diary, 1883–99, concerning work and leisure, especially theatre visits. Berks RO D/EZ98

499. *1883* KINGSBURY, Dorothy, of Norfolk. Diary of travel, including London, *c.*1883–1904. Norfolk RO MC 29 468x

500. *1884* ASHBEE, Charles Robert, of Chipping Camden, Glos, architect and town planner. Diary and papers, 1884–1941. Active in the Art Workers' Guild and the London Survey Comittee. King's Coll Cambridge Modern AC CRA

501. *1884* BOSE, Monoroma, student teacher in London, later teacher at the Victoria School, Lahore. Diary, 1884–5, of student life in London, social activities, sightseeing, Houses of Parliament, Zoo. BLOIO MSS.EUR. F178/69

502. *1884* GODLEE (née SEEBOHM), Juliet, *Lady Godlee*, wife of Sir Rickman John Godlee, surgeon. Diary, 1884–1943, of her domestic life, social engagements, much time spent in London. Available on Women's Language and Experience' mf pt 3 (Adam Matthew, 1996). Suffolk RO (Ipswich) HA 43

503. *1884* LUBBOCK (née FOX-PITT-RIVERS), Alice, *Lady Avebury,* second wife of John Lubbock, 1st Baron Avebury (**371**). Diary, 1884–8. The first part was written retrospectively, describing her courtship and marriage at twenty-two to an older widower. Her domestic life, birth of the children, her husband's work and travels. They took a London house every season. BL Add MSS 62,691

504. *1884* WOODHOUSE, Joseph, of Sheffield, Methodist minister emigrating to Sydney. Diary, 1884, of his journey to a new post in Australia, includes description of his stay in London before sailing. Nat Maritime M MS LIG 140832

505. *1885* CARPENTER, William Boyd, clergyman, Canon of Westminster. Diary, 1885–1917. BL BL Add MSS 46717–65

506. *1885* LASCELLES, *the Hon* Frederica Maria, sister-in-law of 5th Earl of Harewood. Diary, 1885, of family and domestic life. Notes servants' wages and terms of employment. Family health, education of children. Letting of London house. Wigan AS EHC199/M999

507. *1885* SHAW, George Bernard, author and playwright. Diary, 1885–97. LSE R(SR) 293

508. *1885* TURNER, *Mrs* M F Scott, West London, mother of Cecil Scott Turner, *qv.* Diary, 1885–8, covering middle class social engagements, domestic and local events. LMA ACC 1385/1–4

509. *1886* ANON, a member of the ANSON family, of Devon and London. Diary including detailed descriptions of baby care and childhood development of two daughters, 1886–1906. MoL Acc.no.82.267/681–3

510. *1886* BYRON, Margaret Alice, of Nottinghamshire. Diary of travel, including London, 1886–7, 1890–3. Notts Archives DD 704/1–3

511. *1886* CAPELL, *the Hon* Arthur, of Cassiobury Park, Herts, son of 6th Earl of Essex. Diary, 1886–9. Herts ALS D/Z 70 F1–2

512. *1886* COVERNTON, C J, (male) of Heseltine, Powell & Co, stock-jobber. Diary, 1886–7. Guildhall L MS, 23,265

513. *1886* GRIMSTON, Violet, *Countess of Verulam*, of Gorhambury, Herts, wife of 4th Earl of Verulam. Diary, 1886–1936. Herts ALS D/EV F209

514. *1887* DUNN, William, of Newcastle. Diary of travel, including London, 1887. Tyne and Wear AS TWAS 996/1

515. *1887* FLETCHER, Thomas Wayland, of Poplar and Bow, architect. Diary, 1887–1900, social and working life. Extracts in article by MH Port in *East London Papers*, XI (1968). Tower Hamlets LHLA TH/8222

516. *1887* MCEWEN, Daniel, of Southwark, Camberwell and Newington, clerk in office of Official Receivers in Bankruptcy. Diary and accounts, 1887–1911. Active in political societies including Fabian Society, interested in co-operative societies and housing reform. Southwark LSL 1982/11/1

517. *1887* WARD, Thomas Humphrey, journalist with *The Times*. Diary, 1887. UC London MSS ADD 202

518. *1888* LANCHESTER, Charles Compton, of Hannington Rectory, Hants. Diary of visit to London, 1888, at age of eleven. Hants RO 149M71/F1

519. *1888* MOSS, Henry L, of Minnesota, traveller. Diary of European trip, 1888, including London. Minnesota HS P879

520. *1888* WALE, F Lemuel, of Folkestone, Kent, member of Folkestone and Catford Cycling Club. Diary, 1888–94, with cuttings. E Kent AC F/1973/1

521. *1889* ANON, of Oakland, Maine, clergyman, travelling with Mr Roy. Travel diary, 1889, of a journey to England and France, April–June 1889. The London section describes sightseeing trips to Westminster Abbey, St Paul's cathedral, Parliament, the docks, museums and parks. Winterthur M 95/A67

522. *1889* JONES, Emily A, of Brixton and Peckham. Diary, 1889–1900. Social, personal and domestic affairs, excursions. Lambeth AD MS 8/25 (S1655)

523. *1889* RYMER, Samuel Lee, of Croydon, Alderman, and Mayor. Diary for 1889 and 1894, covering his daily activities and, in 1893–4, his official life as Mayor. Croydon LSL Acc 489

524. *1890* MOORE, *Mrs* F D, of Ampfield, Sussex, clergyman's wife. Diary, 30 April–23 June 1890, of journey to visit German eye specialist for her husband's failing eyesight. Stayed in London on the way. Wigan AS EHC139/M924

525. *1890* PEEL, Arthur Wellesley, *1st Viscount Peel*, of Sandy, Beds, politician, Speaker of the House of Commons. Diary, 1890–6. Duke UL

526. *1890* WARD, Dorothy, of Grosvenor Place, daughter of Humphrey Ward and the novelist Mary Ward. Diary, 1890, 1898 of social life, secretarial work for her parents, nursing relatives and, in the 1898 volume, work at the Passmore Edwards Settlement. UC London MSS. Add. 202

527. *1890* WEMYSS (née MORIER), Victoria, *Lady Wester Wemyss*, wife of Rosslyn Erskine Wemyss, Baron Wester Wemyss, Admiral of the Fleet. Diaries, 1890–1926, including London life. Balliol Class H/Box 2, Class N/ Box 12–13

528. *1891* BURT, Septimus, of London. Diary, June 4 1891–Sept 22 1900. LISWA Acc 4859A/73

529. *1891* MOLYNEUX, *the Hon Sir* Richard, of Berkeley Square, Army officer (Major) and courtier. Diary, 1891–1953 (with gaps). Man about town, cultural interests, moved in royal circles. Liverpool RO Molyneux of Sefton

530. *1891* TAIT, Lucy, daughter of Archbishop of Canterbury. Diary, Dec 1891–Dec 1893, Feb 1894–Jan 1897, Nov 1918–Dec 1922, March 1923–Nov 1927, Feb–April 1928. Lambeth Palace L MSS 1605–8

531. *1892* BROMHEAD, Alfred Claude, retired Army officer (Lieutenant-Colonel), and London historian. Diary, 1892–95. ULL MS 963

532. *1892* BROWN, Leonard Joseph, of Shepherd's Bush, railway clerk. Diary, 1892–1939, of day to day activities, work, reading, choir practice, church. Mentions the weather, national news, personal feelings. He worked for the Great Western Railway at Paddington, retiring to Barmouth in 1939, where he continued his diary. Separate notebooks record his mountain-climbing holidays. Nat L Wales 1/292

533. *1893* ANON. Diary of a London gentleman, 1893. Shooting, race meetings, social engagements. Edinburgh UL DK.5.31

534. *1893* DAWSON, Geoffrey, twice Editor of *The Times*. Diary, 1893–1944, with gap 1919–20. Bodleian MS Dawson 1–49

535. *1893* HARVEY, Abraham, of 84 Brooke Road, Hackney, retired City beadle. Diary, 1893–4. Hackney AD M4591/1–2

536. *1893* INGILBY, *Sir* William, of Ripley Castle, Yorks. Diary, 1893–1914 (with gaps) covers his daily life in London. Leeds CL Ingilby records MSS 3600

537. *1893* LEIGHTON, Frederic, *Baron Leighton*, painter. Diary, 1893. R Academy LEI

538. *1893* MANBY, *Mrs*, of Wassell Wood, Worcs. Diary of visit to London, 1893. Worcs RO 705:448, BA3550/2ii

539. *1893* TAIT, Andrew Carlyle, of New Cross and later Ilford. Diary, 1893–4, of his last days at school and first at work, as clerk with James Spicer & Co, stationers and paper merchants, of 50 Thames Street. Extracts in *Victorian Diaries* (ed H Creaton, 2001). Guildhall L MS 20,383

540. *1893* WIDDOWSON, C E, of Isleworth, the family ran a drapery business. Diary, 1893–4. Hounslow LSL LA Archives

541. *1894* HASSALL, John, of Kensington, poster artist. Diary, 1894–1948. Essex UL Hassall Colln

542. *1894* LEVESON GOWER, William George Gresham, clerk in the Parliamentary Office from 1908. Diary, 1894–1918, about personal life and official duties. Parliamentary A Hist Colln

543. *1895* NELSON, Mary E, of Minnesota, traveller. Diary of travel, including London, 1895. Minnesota HS A/N427m

544. *1895* NORMAN, Philip, of the London Survey Committee. Diary, 1895–1931. Business engagements and home life. LMA A/LSC/100–117

545. *1895* ROSE, Eli, of Walthamstow, builder's labourer. Photocopy of diary, 1895, about his working day, the weather, prices, family events and illnesses. Waltham Forest ALSL Acc 8662

546. *1896* HOLDEN, *Sir* Edward Hopkinson, clearing banker, Member of Parliament. Diary, 1896–1916, while Chairman of the London City and Midland Bank, and (1906–10) Member of Parliament for the Heywood Division, Lancashire. HSBC Group Archives

547. *1896* IJAMS, Elizabeth, of Virginia, traveller. Diary of European trip, 1896, including life and entertainment in London. Virginia UL

548. *1896* LOFTUS, Ernest A, of Grays, Essex, Headmaster of Barking Abbey School. Listed in Guinness Book of Records as longest-running living diarist until his death in 1985. He began the diary as a schoolboy and continued it in his post-retirement career as an educational administrator in Africa, 1896–1987. London interest is confined to his period as headmaster of Barking Abbey School, from the 1930s to the 1960s. Thurrock M

549. *1897* BALL, *Sir* William Valentine, of 18 Church Street, South Kensington, barrister, King's Remembrancer. Diary begins in 1891 at age fifteen, but London coverage is from 1897–1900 when studying for the Bar, and 1932–59 as an established and distinguished lawyer. Gregarious social life, with comments on significant contemporaries, political issues, current events and wartime experiences. A Freemason. Private. Mr M Barcroft, 12 Robin Hood Close, Milton Gate, Peterborough PE3 9AR

550. *1897* DOBELL, Eleanor, of Haverstock Hill, and Charing Cross Road, wife of Bertram Dobell, *qv.* Diary, 1897–1909. Bodleian MS Dobell e.35–9, f.4–11

551. *1897* FOOTE, Joseph, of Queensland, Australia, buyer for family company. Diary of voyage to England, including time in London, 1897. Nat Maritime M MS IND/ARC

552. *1897* GIRDLESTONE, F S, chorister of St Paul's cathedral, aged fifteen. Transcript and photocopy of diary, June 1897, concerning preparations for Queen Victoria's Diamond Jubilee. Guildhall L Fo. Pam. 8812

553. *1897* WARREN, Rachel, of Streatham. Diary and other papers, 1897–1903. The diary begins in Rouen at finishing school. From April 1897 it concerns her life in London – theatre, music, social activities, excursions. Public mourning for Queen Victoria and her funeral procession. Entries diminish after Oct 1901. Surrey HC 2377/1a

April 1895 Eli Rose 34 Hazelwood Road Walthamstow Essex

Mon 1st I went up to London this morning by the 5-25 train to Liverpool Street Station: then I walk from there to Bedford Court Mansions Near Bedford Square Thats 40 Minutes walk:

Tues 2nd I am doing A bit of scaffolding at the Bedford Court Mansions with Alfred Hamilton: Working with the plasterer:

Wed 3rd Ditto: My Brother William had A piano come home to day for Kattie

Thur 4th I am working at the Bedford Court Mansions:

Fri 5th Ditto:

Sat 6th The men on the works were I am working Collected for me to day 7-5-4 This evening I have been up high Street to pay my union club money And I went into A little shop and bought A scarfe at 4 3/4 My Wife bought 2 pairs of boots at fishers one pair for Daise price 2-11 & one pair for Jennie price 2-6 I just called in my Brother William and had A class of ginger wine and A bit of cake has it was is Wifes birthday she was 41 years old:

Sunday 7th me & my Wife have been to the Cemetery this afternoon to see the grave were our dear little boy Layes: This evening me & Daise & Kattie have been to St: Michal Church Walthamstow Essex:

5. Eli Rose (**545**) commutes to his building work London in 1895 *(courtesy of Mrs M.A. Shaw and Waltham Forest Archives and Local Studies Library)*

554. *1898* BROWN, Henry Francis, of London, partner in Kilburn, Brown & Co, East India merchants, uncle of Sybil Mary Curtis, *qv.* Diary, 9 June 1898–21 Oct 1909. Social and domestic life, literary and other artistic interests. Wigan AS EHC111/M879

555. *1898* TURNER, Cecil Scott, West London, solicitor, son of Mrs MF Scott Turner, *qv*, Solicitor with Piccadilly firm. Diary, 1898–1956, concentrates on his social life, health, travel and the weather. Resident at Vanderbilt Hotel, Cromwell Road, for over twenty years. Catholic convert. LMA ACC 1385/5–63

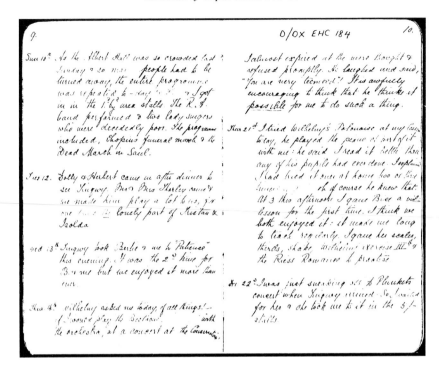

6. Ethel Clementi (**559**) studies music in 1901 *(courtesy of Wigan Archives Service)*

556. *1899* PROCTOR, Robert George Collier, bibliographer in the British Museum. Diary, 1899–1903. BL Add MSS 50190–5

557. *1900* ROSE, George H, of Dalston Gas Company. Diary, 1900–56; access to the post–1914 volumes is restricted. Essex RO Misc Acc D/DK 418/1–57

558. *1901* BIBBINS, *Mrs* Arthur, of Maryland. Diary of visit to London, 1901–2, including opening of Parliament, 1902, and visit to Claydon House. Maryland HS MS 129

559. *1901* CLEMENTI, Ethel, music student. Diary, 3 Jan 1901–26 Feb 1902, with emphasis on her musical interests and education. Lessons, visits to opera, concerts. The latter part concerns her studies in Dresden. Wigan AS D/DX EHC184/M976

560. *1901* COGNEY, *Miss* R D, of East Twickenham. Diary, 1901, mentioning Queen Victoria's funeral, and the Boat Race. Hull UL DX 187/1

561. *1901* FREEMAN, Marjory, of Kingston upon Thames, Surrey. Diary, 1901–3. Kingston MHS KX162/2/1–3

562. *1901* HALE, Edwin, of Battersea. Diary, 1901–8, written for his fiancée, later his wife, during a long engagement. Social activities, work, holidays, anniversaries of their meeting. Wandsworth LHS

563. *1902* ELWELL, Violet, of Australia. Diary of a visit to England, including stays in London from Dec 1902–Feb 1903 and a later visit in July 1905, before her return to Australia. Detailed and perceptive descriptions of her impressions, traffic, tube travel, entertainments. Private. Currently being edited for publication by Ruth Longford (cotignac@hotmail.com).

564. *1902* FITZWILLIAMS, Gerard Hall Lloyd, medical practitioner (surgeon). Diary, 1902–68. Nat L Wales See NLW Ann Rept 1976–7 p.68

565. *1902* NICOLL, T Vere, medical practitioner. Diary of London doctor, 1902–19. Everday life, patients, social engagements, family matters. Wellcome GC/133

566. *1902* SAMUEL, *Sir* Marcus, later *1st Viscount Bearsted*, Lord Mayor of London, joint founder of Shell Transport & Trading Co. Diary, 1902–3, of his mayoral year, with personal material. Guildhall L MS 10,590

567. *1904* HEELAS, Newton, of Norbiton, clergyman, Vicar of St Peter's, Norbiton. Diary, 1904–38. He became Vicar of St Peter's in 1916 and retired due to ill-health in 1937. Kingston MHS KX173/1/1/1–30

568. *1904* RICH, Samuel Morris, lay minister of South London Liberal Jewish Synagogue. Diary, 1904–49. Southampton UL MS 168

569. *1905* BARNARD, Ettwell A B, of Worcestershire, antiquary. Diary of a cycle tour, including London, 1905. Worcs RO 705:673, BA5821/1–3

570. *1905* COKAYNE, Mary Dorothea, of Putney, wife of G E Cokayne, and mother of Brien Cokayne, *qqv*. Diary, 1905. Very detailed on everyday events. Northants RO C 664

571. *1905* WRENCH, *Sir* John Evelyn, founder of the English Speaking Union. Pocket diary, 1905, covering day to day life in London. BL Add MSS 59,557

572. *1906* HOLMES, *Sir* Charles John, director of the National Gallery, and National Portrait Gallery. Diary, 1906–35. Nat Portrait G MS 26

573. *1906* PHILLIPS, Ruth, Secretary to Lucien Wolf and Israel Zangwill. Diary, 1906–8. Southampton UL AJ/9

574. *1907* CURTIS, Sybil Mary, of Westminster, niece of Henry Francis Brown, *qv*. Diary, 20 Jan 1907–27 Feb 1910, with gaps. Her active work as a parishioner of St Margaret's, Westminster, charitable activities, Westminster Abbey, social and domestic life, mention of suffragettes, feminists. Wigan AS D/DZ EHC106/M874

575. *1907* WATERS, Amy L, of the United States, traveller. Diary of a European tour, June–Sept 1907, with a stay in London, sightseeing, theatre visits. New York PL

576. *1907* WILLIAMS, George Howard, of Hitchcock, Williams & Co, drapers, St Paul's Churchyard and soldier (Sergeant, RAMC). Diary, 1907–61 relating to his work with the family firm, First World War service, much of which was at the 3rd London General Hospital in Wandsworth, later career and holidays. Little of London relevance after 1919. IWM GWH/1–66

577. *1908* BLACKEBY, Robert James, of 29 Christchurch Buildings, Lisson Street NW1, shop employee. Diary, 1908–46. He worked for the department store Peter Robinson Ltd. Minutiae of his daily doings, including mealtimes and weekly list of his domestic washing. A Sunday School teacher. He notes expenses and post received daily. WCA Acc 1489

578. *1908* DEAKIN, Phyllis, journalist on *The Times*, founder-member Women's Press Club. Diary and papers, 1908–96. Fawcett L 7/PAD

579. *1908* SMYTH, Mary Louisa, of Edworth, Beds. Diary of visit to London, 1908. Beds RO SM/E 54

580. *1911* ADDIS, *Sir* Charles Stewart, banker, financial adviser and negotiator. Addis's long-running diary began in 1881, but the early part of his career was spent in the Far East. In 1911 he was promoted to the London branch of the Hong Kong and Shanghai Bank. SOAS PP MS 14

581. *1911* COKAYNE, Brien, later *Lord Cullen of Ashbourne*, banker, Governor of the Bank of England. Diary, 1911–29, of social and working life. Many ephemera glued in. Northants RO X1344; C1345–61

582. *1911* LEFTWICH, Joseph, of East London, furrier's apprentice, and poet. Diary, 1911, of eighteen-year old Jewish apprentice belonging to the 'East London Group' of writers and artists, friend of Isaac Rosenberg. The diary mainly concerns the author's cultural and political pursuits. Includes the Young Socialist League, rallies, the Bethnal Green by-election, and strikes including the London schoolchildren's strike in Sept. WM P351

583. *1911* REITH, John Charles Walsham, *Baron Reith*, Director-General BBC, cabinet minister. Diary, 1911–71. BBC WA S60

584. *1912* GROSVENOR, Eliza Francis, of 75 Oakley St, Chelsea, widow. Diary, 21 March–4 Sept 1912, entitled 'diary written on scraps of paper'. Difficult to read, concentrates on her daily life in Chelsea with her three sons. Wigan AS EHC161/M946

585. *1912* TERRERO, *Mrs* J, suffragist. Diary, 1912, including time served in Hollway Prison. MoL 50.82/1116

586. *1913* DALE, Douglas, of Streatham, screenwriter. Diary, 1913–15, relating to his family life at 41 Stanhope Road, Streatham, as a teenager, and 1923–5 relating to his social engagements around London. Lambeth AD IV/147/2/1–6

587. *1913* HARRADENCE, W E, (male) of Upper Norwood, antiquarian. Diary, 8 Aug 1913–1 Nov 1913. Daily activities and his interests. Includes theatre programmes and other ephemera. Wigan AS EHC151/M936

588. *1913* NORMAN, Montagu Collet, *Baron Norman*, banker. Photocopied diary, 1913–44. Bank of England

589. *1914* ANON, (female) of Kensington. Diary, July 23–September 5 1914, recording the preliminaries to and outbreak of the First World War as it impinged on her comfortable social circle in London. Interesting for rumours and scare-stories as well as food shortages, shopping and travel problems. IWM Misc 29/522

590. *1914* BRITTAIN, F, (male) soldier (nursing orderly, RAMC). Transcription of diary, 1914–19, of which Dec 1914–Aug 1915 covers his service at the 2nd London General Military Hospital, Chelsea, before being sent overseas. IWM 99/55/1

591. *1914* BUNBURY, Edith Marjorie, of Holborn, and Peckham, charity worker. Diary, 1914–15, in two notebooks. The first, covering July–Sept 1914, is very personal with much self-analysis and criticism; the second, Sept 1914–Nov 1915 is a diary of the progress of the war, with a few personal reactions, insights and anecdotes. LMA B00/035

592. *1914* COULES, *Miss* M, daughter of news editor at Reuters Press Agency. Diary, June 1914–Nov 1915. Outbreak of war, role of press, work with Belgian refugees, Zeppelin raids. IWM 97/25/1

593. *1914* CUBITT, Ada Alice, of Norfolk. Diary of visit to London, 1914. Norfolk RO FX 1/2

594. *1914* DOBBS, Rosalind, sister of Catherine, Lady Courtney, *qv*. Diary of the Great War, 1914–*c*.1916. LSE Courtney Colln XL/1

595. *1914* HOBBS, *Sir* Joseph John Talbot, Australian Army officer (Lieutenant-General). First World War diary (copy), including accounts of the London victory marches. Australian WM PR82/153

596. *1914* LOURIE, Dora Leba, of the United States, traveller. Diary covering 9 July–25 Aug 1914, when she was visiting Europe with the Polytechnic Touring Association. Describes short stay in London before travelling to France and Switzerland. Mention of suffragettes. U Westminster Archives Acc 1999/5

597. *1914* MCPHEE, J E, Australian Army soldier (Sergeant). Diary, 1914–18, including leave parties to London. Australian WM 3DRL/2610

598. *1914* MEYSEY-THOMPSON, H C, Army officer (Captain, King's Rifle Corps). Diary, 1914–19. He enlisted in the Inns of Court OTC in Aug 1914 and trained with them before being commissioned and serving in France. Badly wounded at the third Battle of Ypres, moved to a London hospital from June 1918–May 1919. IWM 92/19/1

599. *1914* ROSENBAUM, Edward, librarian of British Library of Political and Economic Science. Diary, 1914–60. LSE Misc Colln 638

600. *1914* TOWER, *Miss* W L B, helper at Londonderry House Hospital. Miss Tower was in London in Oct 1914, and Sept 1915–16. Her diary describes London's precautions against air attack, Zeppelin raids, and her service as a hospital helper. IWM P472

601. *1915* ATKINSON, R B, regular soldier (29th Divisional Cyclist Company). Diary transcript, April 1915–May 1916. Mainly his Gallipoli service, but invalided home for treatment at Southwark Military Hospital Jan–May 1916. IWM 95/1/1

602. *1915* DICK, Arthur Morrison, Australian Army soldier (Sergeant). Diary of his war service, 1915–19, including a trip to London on leave with the 5th Brigade football team. Australian WM PR00187

603. *1915* HENDY, P G, Australian Army soldier (Driver). Diary, 1915–19, of war service including leave in London. Australian WM PR84/144

604. *1915* MOORE, Ralph Ingram, Australian Army officer (Captain). Diary, 1915–16 of his service at Gallipoli, evacuation to England with enteric fever, leave in London including ANZAC day celebrations there in 1916. Australian WM PR88/206

605. *1915* PELLY, A R, Army officer (Captain, Norfolk Regiment). Diary, 1915, including treatment for wounds at Lady Evelyn Mason's Officers' Hospital in London, Sept–Dec 1915. IWM 91/15/1

606. *1915* RIXON, A J, of Lambeth, soldier (Company Sergeant Major, London Irish Rifles). CSM Rixon's transcribed diary (1915–16) records his service on the Western Front, but includes a period of home leave in Lambeth in Aug 1915. IWM 99/13/1

607. *1915* TREDGETT, Madeleine, of Croydon. Child's diary (photocopy) of lessons, church-going, outings and amusements, 1915–17. Cambridge CRO R93/47

608. *1916* COOPER, Frank Simpson, soldier (NZ Expeditionary Force). Diary of his war service, 1914–18, of which the entries for 1916–18 relate to leave in London and other parts of England, visiting relatives, going to the theatre and restaurants. Canterbury UL MS 35

609. *1916* ENNOR, F H, Army officer (Subaltern, Grenadier Guards). Diary, Jan 1916–March 1918. Military training in Romford, April–Nov 1916, and service in London with the Grenadier Guards, Dec 1916–July 1917. IWM 86/28/2

610. *1916* FOULKES-ROBERTS, Arthur, of Denbigh and London, solicitor. Diary, 1916–46. Denbighs RO (Ruthin branch)

611. *1916* HARRIS, R E, of New Zealand, soldier (Rifleman). Photocopy of diary, July–Nov 1916 of life in the trenches, hospital treatment and then leave in London. IWM 86/66/1

612. *1917* CORBOULD, William W, Australian Army soldier (Gunner). Diary, 1917–20, of his wartime service including spells of leave in London. Australian WM PR83/245

613. *1917* GEE, Harry Alfred, Australian Army soldier (Sapper). Diary, 1917–19, of his war service including leave in London. Australian WM PR00378

614. *1917* HOLGATE, Thomas, soldier (London Rifle Brigade). Diary, 1917, including time in London. Manchester ALS Misc/1032

615. *1917* MADDISON, Robert, Australian Army soldier (Private). Diary of war service, 1917–18, including leave in London. Australian WM PR84/213

616. *1917* MERCER, Harold, Australian Army soldier. Diary, 1917–18, concerning his duties with the Salvage Corps in France, and hospitalisation in London. State L NSW MSS 1143

March

Sunday 21th. Went to church in the morning & met Aunt Soie, who spent the day. To=morrow=day is my

CONFIRMATION DAY.

The Bishop of Croydon confirmed me. Dadda, Mother & Aunt Flo (my godparents) gave me a beautiful white prayer=book. & Aunt Soie a lovely gold cross & chain. Mr King also sent me a book called the "Daily Round". & another little book "Just Confirmed" I was Confirmed with a friend of Winnie's (Edith Carter).

Monday. Went to school all day. Dadda is working in London now

Tuesday. Went to school all day.

Wednesday 24th Went to school in the morning, & for an hour in the afternoon, at quarter to five, I went to church with John & mother, At half-past six, I went to the last Confirmation Class, (it wasn't really a confirmation class, but one to prepare you Holy for communion) The Vicar gave us all a little book to-day, it is adapted from the Scouts Prayerbook, & very nice indeed.

Thursday 25th I went to school in the morning, & in the afternoon I went to Grandpa's with Mother, Auntie & John, because there was a Mothers Union Service too which mother, aunt F. & Great=Aunt=Ellen were going to.

Friday 26th Went to school all day, mother & Auntie went down the town, so I hurried home & laid the tea.

Saturday 27th Went to the cemetry & (put) put some flowers on Mr King's mother's grave, we went to Grandpa's for dinner, as it was his birthday, (had a pig's head for dinner) went to the library as we came home.

Sunday 28th Went to church in the morning & sat afterwards with Dadda, Winnie & I went together this afternoon.

Monday 29th To school in the morning & in the afternoon I had my photograph taken in my Confirmation dress & veil, This is a secret for Dadda on Easter Day.

7. Madeleine Tredgett (**607**) records an eventful day in Croydon in 1915 *(courtesy of Mrs M. E. Cooke and Cambridgeshire Archives Service)*

617. *1917* PEILE, *Mrs* L, of Margate, housewife. Diary of life in Margate with young daughter, 1916–17 with German air and sea attack, includes stay in a West End hospital in Sept 1917 during the 'Harvest Moon' raids. IWM 94/2/1

618. *1917* POTTER, H B, of the Harvard Surgical Unit, US Army doctor. Captain Potter served in France and most of his diary, 1916–17, deals with that experience, but en route back to the USA in June 1917 he visited London hospitals. IWM 80/17/1

619. *1917* RUSH, Jessie, of Shepherds Bush. Transcript of her diary, 1917–19, 1921, of everyday life during and after the Great War. Hammersmith ALHC H920 RUS

620. *1917* SMITH, *Miss* C, WAAC. Photocopy of her diary account of the first few days of her WAAC service in London in June 1917, mentioning her living conditions, initial training, and Zeppelin raids. IWM 98/9/1

621. *1917* TURTLE, Florence, of Wimbledon Park, department store book and stationery buyer. Diary 1917–80 (with gaps) of her work and social life. Food, drink, evening classes, entertainments. Wandsworth LHS

622. *1917* WATKINSON, W E, Lieutenant, Rifle Brigade. Diary, 1917, including hospital treatment at Lady Northcliffe's Hospital, London, Oct–Dec 1917. IWM 90/28/1

623. *1918* ALWIN, Owen, printer. Diary, 1918–50. Bodleian MS Eng. misc. e.2410–21

624. *1918* BIDDLECOMBE, Kathleen, of 6 Cobbett Road, Eltham. Diary, 1918, aged fourteen, recording her life at home, looking after the house and doing the shopping, while her parents worked at the Royal Arsenal, Woolwich. Greenwich LHL MSS BIDD

625. *1918* KEATING, Noel Michael, Australian Army soldier (Corporal). Diary, 1918, of military staff clerk about his war service, including return to London after end of the war for duty with demobilisation staff. Australian WM PR00561

626. *1918* KENYON, *Miss* W L, VAD nurse. The complete diary covers her war service from 1914–18 in France and the UK; only the section for Feb–Oct 1918 deals with London, when she was a military VAD at King George's Hospital. Transcript. IWM 84/24/1

627. *1918* LEACH, Cyril Henry, of 18 Gayton Road, Harrow, insurance company employee. Diary, 1918–70, covering his social life and some references to his work at the Northern Assurance Company. Harrow LHC A6/2

628. *1918* SORRELL, J, Australian Army officer (Lieutenant). Diary of war service, including training in London. Australian WM 2DRL/0427

629. *1919* BUDD, G A F, of Oxfordshire. Diary of visit to London, 1919. Oxfordshire Archives Misc.Budd.XIII/3

630. *1919* MILES, Dorothy, of 33 Cuthbert Road, Waddon, Surrey, secretary. Diary, 1919, when she was a secretary at LH Turtle (toolmaker and cutler) of Crown Hill, Croydon. Her working and social life including her engagement, the peace celebrations, railway strike, departure of fiancé for Australia. Croydon LSL AR18

631. *1920* BENSINGER, Ruth, of 7 Dartmouth Road, NW2, schoolgirl. Diary, 1920–6, 1928. Ruth lived with her parents and brother ('Boysie') and attended South Hampstead High School. Lively entries record her life at school, visits to friends, family and synagogue, and holiday trips to see relations in Germany. MoL 97.100

632. *1921* EVANS, Albert, Member of Parliament for Islington West and South West. Diary, 1921–75, brief entries cover domestic and trade matters (he was a member of the Goldsmiths, Jewellers and Allied Trades Association) and his period as an MP for Islington West (1947–50, and Islington South West, 1950–70). Islington LHC YL 310 Evans

633. *1921* LANGFORD, Gladys, of Highbury, schoolteacher. Diary, 1921–69, about her domestic, social and teaching life, including air raids, rationing, concerts, and VE Day celebrations in the Second World War years. Many references to her reading. Islington LHC YX 079 LAN

634. *1922* ST JOHN, Henry Algernon Francis, of Acton, local government finance officer. Diary, 1922–68, with cuttings, photographs and other ephemera relating to an uneventful life. Minutiae of daily life, sometimes quite intimate, written with a self-conscious eye on posterity. Some comments on political events. Ealing LHL Acc 68

635. *1923* HOOPER, Hilda, of City of London Girls' School, schoolteacher (art). Diary, 1923–61, brief personal entries with little on the school itself. Lambeth AD Misc IV/72

636. *1923* NEVINSON, John Lea, costume historian. Diary, 12 May 1923–25 Dec 1980, of his work at the Victoria and Albert Museum, later at the Ministry of Education, and early retirement from 1961. Social life, cultural interests. S Antiq 911/3/1–118

637. *1923* ANON. Diary, 1923–4, kept at Staplehurst, Kent, includes visits to London, concerts. New York PL

638. *1924* OSBORNE, *Sir* Francis D'Arcy, *Bart*, later *12th Duke of Leeds*, diplomat. Diary of life in London, 1924–6 and a fuller diary for 1926, relating to a period in London. Social engagements, theatre visits, family, hobbies. Many other volumes cover his extensive service abroad. BL Egerton 3830–3

639. *1926* CHAMPNESS, *Sir* William Henry, lawyer, HM Lieutenant of City, liveryman, sheriff. Diary of personal matters, 1926–38, with autobiographical notes 1873–1925. Guildhall Library also has the journals of his years as under-sheriff (1928–9) and sheriff (1937–8) of the City. Guildhall L MS 14,765/1–6

640. *1928* HEAP, Anthony, St Pancras, local government officer. Diary, 1928–85. Heap worked for the department store Peter Robinson Ltd until 1940, then became a local government officer with St Pancras (later Camden) for the rest of his working life. Diary covers work, health, social life and especially theatre, cinema and TV performances. He contributed reviews to the NALGO house magazine for a period. Visited Festival of Britain. LMA ACC 2243

641. *1928* WILLMOTT, Herbert M, of 16 Langham Mansions, London SW5, retired civil engineer. Diary for 1928–47 covers his retirement life in Earls Court including service as ARP warden in Second World War in Kensington. His interests included the church, the League of Nations Union, the Charity Organisation Society, and the theatre. Concerns about rationing, and his health. LMA F/WLM/8–27

642. *1929* LUMSDEN (née HUGHES), A J, (female) of London and Steeple Aston, Wilts. Diary, 1929–35, 1952–80. Wilts RO Misc 3523

643. *1930* RITCHLEY, William G, of Bexley, local government officer. Diary, 1930–72, including his work in Town Clerk's Dept, Bexley. Bexley LSAC PE/RIT/1–43

644. *1931* DON, Alan Campbell, clergyman. Diary, 12 May 1931–25 Dec 1946. Chaplain and Secretary to Archbishop Lang, a Chaplain to the King, Speaker's Chaplain, Canon of Westminster and Rector of St Margaret's Westminster. Lambeth Palace L MS 2861–71

645. *1931* MARTINDALE, Louisa, medical practitioner (cancer specialist). Diary, Jan–April 1931. Everyday life, patients, social engagements. Other volumes cover foreign travel. Wellcome MSS 3482

646. *1931* WITHINGTON, Alan, railway employee, of Highgate. Personal diaries, 1931–98 of his life in Highgate. Lengthy daily entries with many photographs attached. HLSI

647. *1932* BOULT, *Sir* Adrian Cedric, conductor. Diary, 1928–81, of professional and social engagements. BBC WA S32/1–44

648. *1932* MUSPRATT, Rosamonde, wife of Sydney Muspratt, Indian Army officer. Diary of family and social life in England, 1932–33. The family lived near Maidenhead, but Mrs Muspratt visited London at least once a week for shopping and social engagements. BLOIO MSS.EUR. F223/73–4

649. *1934* GOODLETT, Alexander Kay, of Acton, bank clerk, and PLA river emergency warden. Diary, 1934–40, a transcript, edited by his brother. Home life with parents, wartime work, bomb damage, transport problems. Ealing LHL

650. *1934* HALL, Edward, of Barnsley and Surbiton, diary-collector, father of Joan Mary Hall, *qv*. Diary, 17 Dec 1934–24 April 1935; 4 Aug–9 Aug 1936; 23 Oct–25 Nov 1937; 22 May 1938– 10 Jan 1939. The diaries cover his move from Barnsley to Surbiton, his financial problems, and his career as a second-hand bookseller. Wigan AS EHC88/M855–6

651. *1934* HEITLAND, Beryl C, of 46 Crouch Hill. Diary, Feb 1934–Feb 1935, with much on her garden and its progress. Islington LHC YX HEI

652. *1935* KITCHIN, Kenneth, of Stationers' School, schoolboy (sixth-former). Diary in verse, 1935–6, about daily life in Hornsey and Muswell Hill. Transcript. Extracts in *Hornsey Historical Society Bulletin* no.28 (1987). Hornsey HS

653. *1936* BREED, Clara Mona, of New York, traveller. Diary kept on visits to England, 1936–7, and 1939. New York PL

654. *1936* HALL, Joan Mary, later ENDERS, of Surbiton, schoolgirl, daughter of Edward Hall, *qv.* Diary of school and home life, 1936–7. Wigan AS EHC224–9/RM1575

655. *1936* LEASK, *Mrs* D, of Crouch End, housewife. Diary (edited transcript), 1936–50, kept at family home in Crouch End before marriage in 1937, then at various homes until return to London at the end of the war. Material on cultural interests, the air raids, food shortages, V-weapons and post-war austerities. IWM 97/28/1

656. *1936* WRIGLEY, W R, of Upper Tooting. Diary, 1936–9, 1941–5, but from 1942 he was serving with the RAF away from London. He was in Tooting during the Blitz. IWM 76/10/1

657. *1937* BEARUP, Thomas William, London representative of the Australian Broadcasting Commission. Diary, 1937–51, 1959–62, while working in London. Australian NL MS 7290

658. *1937* KAYE, Colin C, of Larchmont, New York, traveller. Diary of a European tour, May–Oct 1937, with sightseeing trip in London. New York PL

659. *1937* TYLER, Violet Gladys, of Ladywell Road, Lewisham, office worker. Diary, 1937–41. She lived with her parents, worked at Maltina Bakeries, Blackfriars Road. Family and working life, the weather, Blitz experiences. Lewisham LSC A98/9/1–5

660. *1937* VEAZEY, *Mrs* J, of Sutton, and South East London, clergyman's wife. Diary of life at home with family in Sutton, Aug 1937–Aug 1940, and in South East London, Sept 1940–Aug 1945. Reactions to Munich crisis, outbreak of war, air raids, V-weapons. Extracts in *People at War, 1939–45* by M. Moynihan (1974). IWM PP/MCR/199

661. *1938* ANDREWS, Sylvia M, schoolteacher. Photocopied diary extracts, 1938–45, interspersed with letters from her brother. She was evacuated to Tonbridge, Kent, but made visits to London. IWM 88/50/1

662. *1938* HALL, Vivienne, typist. Diary of the Munich crisis, Sept–Oct 1938, continued intermittently from 1939–45, recording reactions to the outbreak of war, air raids generally, the Blitz and V-weapons. IWM Con Shelf DS/MISC/88 and 84/35/1A

663. *1938* MORRISON-BELL, Sheila, secretary. Diary, Sept–Oct 1938, while working in London, recording her reactions to the Munich crisis. IWM 91/12/1

664. *1938* STEPHEN, *Sir* James Alexander, *Bart*, ARP warden, AA soldier. Diary, 1938–45, beginning with the Munich crisis. Author had mental health problems, had difficulty finding war work, eventually becoming an ARP warden, then Ack-Ack gunner at Woolwich until discharged on medical grounds in May 1942. In countryside for rest of the war, continuing diary until 1945. IWM P264

665. *1939* ANON, (male) of Highams Park, London E4, civil servant. Diary, 1939–41. M-O Diarist 5039.9

666. *1939* ANON, (female) of Leyton, London E17, bookkeeper. Diary, Aug–Nov 1939. M-O Diarist 5437

667. *1939* ANON, (female) of London N5, schoolteacher and reporter. Diary, Aug–Sept 1939. Extract (with pseudonym 'June Chivers') in *Mass Observation Diaries: an Introduction,* comp. S Haines (1991). M-O Diarist 5350

668. *1939* ANON, (female) of London N6, and Northampton, art student. Diary, 1939–40, 1943. M-O Diarist 5352

669. *1939* ANON, (female) of London N6, schoolteacher and ARP ambulance attendant. Diary, 1939–40. M-O Diarist 5422

670. *1939* ANON, (male) of London NW1, and Thrapston, Northants, master printer. Diary, Sept 1939–Feb 1940. M-O Diarist 5209

671. *1939* ANON, (female) of London NW1 and NW8, medical practitioner (psychiatrist). Diary, 1939–41. Extract (with pseudonym 'Rachel Schultz') in *Mass Observation Diaries: an Introduction*, comp. S Haines (1991). M-O Diarist 5280

672. *1939* ANON, (female) of Cricklewood, London NW2, housewife. Diary, Aug–Oct 1939. Extract in *Wartime Women* (ed D Sheridan, 1990). M-O Diarist 5336

673. *1939* ANON, (female) of London NW3, and Taunton, Somerset, schoolteacher (history). Diary, Sept 1939. Extract (with pseudonym 'Ella Taylor') in *Mass Observation Diaries: an Introduction*, comp. S Haines (1991). M-O Diarist 5315

674. *1939* ANON, (male) of London NW3, and Cambridge, student, and research physicist. Diary, Sept 1939. M-O Diarist 5187

675. *1939* ANON, (female) of London NW3, actress. Diary, 1939–42, 1946–7, 1953. Extract (with pseudonym 'Dorothea Jones') in *Mass Observation Diaries: an Introduction*, comp. S Haines (1991). M-O Diarist 5250

676. *1939* ANON, (female) of London NW9, and Great Missenden, Bucks, retired schoolteacher. Diary, 1939–45. M-O Diarist 5402

677. *1939* ANON, (female) of London NW11, and Warminster, Wilts, architectural assistant. Diary, 1939–43. M-O Diarist 5425

678. *1939* ANON, (female) of Blackheath, London SE3, housewife. Diary, 1939–43. Extract (with pseudonym 'Rose Brown') in *Mass Observation Diaries: an Introduction*, comp. S Haines (1991). M-O Diarist 5342

679. *1939* ANON, (female) of London SE4, civil servant. Diary, 1939–42. M-O Diarist 5278

680. *1939* ANON, (male) of Eltham, London SE9, park keeper. Diary, 1939–43. M-O Diarist 5163

681. *1939* ANON, (female) of London SE26, journalist. Diary, 1939–40, 1944. M-O Diarist 5349

682. *1939* ANON, (male) of Streatham, London SW2, university student, and in HM Forces. Diary, 1939–43. M-O Diarist 5061.1

683. *1939* ANON, (male) of London SW11, and Cambridge, student. Diary, Aug–Sept 1939. M-O Diarist 5086

684. *1939* ANON, (male) of London SW11, film strip producer. Diary, 1939–40, 1942–4, 1946. M-O Diarist 5275

685. *1939* ANON, (male) of Barnes, London SW13, and Birmingham, buyer. Diary, 1939–45. M-O Diarist 5132

686. *1939* ANON, (female) of East Sheen, London SW14, ARP warden (part-time). Diary, Sept 1939, Aug–Sept 1941. M-O Diarist 5362

687. *1939* ANON, (male) of London SW14, store research director. Diary, 1939–40. M-O Diarist 5136

688. *1939* ANON, (male) of Merton, London SW19, civil servant. Diary, Sept 1939. M-O Diarist 5120

689. *1939* ANON, (male) of London SW19, author and journalist. Diary, Sept–Dec 1939, Jan–Aug 1941. M-O Diarist 5193.1

690. *1939* ANON, (male) of London W2, clerk. Diary, Aug 1939. M-O Diarist 5011

691. *1939* ANON, (female) of London W2, journalist and writer. Diary, 1939–40. M-O Diarist 5291

692. *1939* ANON, (male) of London W3, chemist. Diary, 1939–40. M-O Diarist 5101

693. *1939* ANON, (female) of London W4, social worker. Diary, 1939–40. M-O Diarist 5382

694. *1939* ANON, (female) of Ealing, London W5, and Lymington, Hants, civil servant (unemployed). Diary, Aug–Dec 1939, June–Aug 1940. Extract (with pseudonym 'Janet Watson') in *Mass Observation Diaries: an Introduction*, comp. S Haines (1991). M-O Diarist 5269

695. *1939* ANON, (male) of Ealing, London W5, West Looe, Cornwall, and Cheltenham, Glos, postal sorter. Diary, 1939–47. M-O Diarist 5089

696. *1939* ANON, (male) of London W5, assistant solicitor, local government. Diary, Aug–Sept 1939. M-O Diarist 5012

697. *1939* ANON, (male) of London W7, office worker. Diary, Aug 1939, May 1940. M-O Diarist 5092

698. *1939* ANON, (female) of London W9, proprietor of Leacroft Service Bureau. Diary, Dec 1939–March 1940. M-O Diarist 5356

699. *1939* ANON, (female) of London W10, housewife. Diary, Sept 1939. M-O Diarist 5262

700. *1939* ANON, (male) of Ealing, London W13, architect's assistant. Diary, 1939–40. M-O Diarist 5237

701. *1939* ANON, (female) of Beckenham, Kent, and London, schoolteacher. Diary, 1941–2. M-O Diarist 5412

702. *1939* ANON, (female) of Beckenham, Kent, researcher into viral diseases. Diary, Aug–Sept 1939. M-O Diarist 5456

703. *1939* ANON, (female) of Croydon, Surrey, and Cambridge, housewife. Diary, 1939–40. M-O Diarist 5366

704. *1939* ANON, (female) of Croydon, Surrey, civil servant. Diary, Sept–Oct 1939, June 1940. M-O Diarist 5383

705. *1939* ANON, (male) of Eastcote, Middx, master decorator. Diary, 1939–41. M-O Diarist 5129

706. *1939* ANON, (male) of Hayes, Middx, estimator on airframe contracts. Diary, 1939–41, 1943. M-O Diarist 5032

707. *1939* ANON, (male) of Ilford, Essex, accountant. Diary, Sept 1939. M-O Diarist 5042

708. *1939* ANON, (male) of Kingston-upon-Thames, Surrey, clerk. Diary, 1939–41. M-O Diarist 5170

709. *1939* ANON, (female) of London, and Corfe Castle, Dorset, housewife and civil servant. Diary, 1939–45, with some gaps. M-O Diarist 5478

710. *1939* ANON, (female) of Purley, Surrey, assistant organiser of local Care Committee. Diary, Aug 1939, Sept–Dec 1940. M-O Diarist 5246

711. *1939* ANON, (male) of Richmond, Surrey, and Dalton-in-Furness, Lancs, civil servant. Diary, Sept 1939–March 1940. M-O Diarist 5135

712. *1939* ANON, (female) of Romford, Essex, schoolgirl, pupil teacher. Diary, Sept 1939. Extract in *Wartime Women* (ed D Sheridan 1990). M-O Diarist 5370

713. *1939* ANON, (male) of Sanderstead, Surrey, engineer's draughtsman. Diary, Aug 1939, June–July 1940. M-O Diarist 5155

714. *1939* ANON, (male) of Sidcup, Kent, bank clerk. Diary, Aug–Sept 1939. M-O Diarist 5141

715. *1939* ALLAN, *Miss* M E, staff journalist on the *Daily Herald*, later war correspondent. Diary covering the first half of 1939 in London. IWM 95/8/7

716. *1939* BROWNE, Thomas Edward, of 75 Casimir Road, Hackney, ARP warden. Diary, September 1939–May 1945. Daily work as air raid warden, dealing with incidents, problems with rota, everyday life. Hackney AD D/F/BRO/1/1–7

717. *1939* BULLARD, B C, WAAF (Flight Officer). The diary covers 1939–45. She was in London in the autumn of 1941, serving as a cipher clerk at SOE, Baker Street, and from Sept 1942 successively at the Air Ministry, Bush House, Transport Command, Harrow and RAF Hendon. Much is about her social life, but she also describes air raids in Feb 1944 and the V-weapon attacks. IWM 86/46/1

718. *1939* CARVER, *Miss* N V, of West Norwood, supervisor at Central Telegraph Office. Diary, 23 Aug 1939–31 Dec 1945, of her wartime experiences in London, ARP measures, civilian conditions, D-Day, VE and VJ Days, the Blitz and V-weapons, with graphic descriptions of bomb damage in the City and near her suburban home. IWM 90/16/1

719. *1939* CHAVE, *Dr* S P W, of Upper Norwood, laboratory assistant. The diary transcript runs from Oct 1939 to June 1942, recording war news and the effect of the Blitz on Upper Norwood and the West End, conditions on the Home Front, and his work at the Emergency Public Health Laboratory. IWM 79/27/1

720. *1939* COMYNS, Mary, of Uvedale Road, Enfield, schoolgirl, pupil at Enfield County School. Diary, 1939–45, of daily life during the Second World War. Enfield LHU 942.1893

721. *1939* COTTON, *Mrs* E H, of the United States, resident in London, and Devon. Transcript of her diary covering life in Britain during the Second World War, particularly her residence in Swiss Cottage. Civilian conditions, Anglo-American relations, the Blitz and V-weapons. IWM 93/3/1

722. *1939* COX, Gwladys, of West Hampstead, housewife. Transcript of a war diary, starting 3 Sept 1939 and ending 8 May 1945. She was bombed out in Oct 1940. Excellent description of life during the Blitz, civilian conditions, shortages, rationing and the V-weapon raids. IWM 86/46/1 (P) Original in NLW

723. *1939* EUSTACE, *Mrs* C, of Chiswick, Scout leader. Photocopied diary, Sept 1939–Sept 1944, of her work as an Assistant District Commissioner for the Scout movement and her involvement with the 8th Chiswick Pack. Describes how the war affected scouting in general, and her pack in particular. IWM 83/27/1

724. *1939* GODDARD, *Miss* V, of Earl's Court. Transcript of diary, 1939–43, of her family's experiences of the outbreak of war, ARP, rationing, the Blitz and bomb damage. IWM Con Shelf

725. *1939* GOLDEN, Grace, artist. Diary, 1939–54, of her life in London including her work as a war artist. MoL Ac. 93.158 (Grace Golden archive)

726. *1939* KING, F R, RN officer (Lieutenant). Photocopy of his diary for Aug 1939–Jan 1940 covers his service with No. 101 stretcher-bearers in London; from 1941–5 he was with the Naval Training Film Section in London, and wrote mainly about his social life among the artistic fringe. IWM 81/5/1

727. *1939* LAWRENCE, Marie Roma, of Townshend Terrace, Richmond, local government secretary. Diary, 1939–45, of her life in wartime Richmond. She lived with her parents, worked as secretary to the parks superintendant. Wide interests, including playing the clarinet. Richmond LC

728. *1939* LAWS (née HOWARD), Mary, nurse at Hendon Cottage Hospital. Diary, 1939–41 about her life and work in the early part of the war. She left to marry in 1941. IWM 73/54/1

729. *1939* MEADER, Anne Isabella. Diary, Sept 1939–April 1946. Typescript. Bodleian MS Eng. misc. *c*.569–74

730. *1939* MILES, Constance, of Shere, Surrey, journalist and housewife. Diary of wartime life, 1939–43, of a fifty-eight year old housewife and journalist, including visits to London. IWM 99/74/1

731. *1939* MOTT, *Miss* H P L, of Teddington, and Greenwich. Diary of her life in Teddington, 1939–46, and Greenwich, 1946–51, recording her reactions to world events and politics as well as day to day life. IWM 97/14/3

732. *1939* PANTING, Horace, of East London, schoolteacher (science). Diary, 1939–40, relating to the evacuation of Holborn Boys' School to Wiltshire. I Education DC/HP DC 02,03,05/98

733. *1939* PENNY, Henry A, of Paddington, bus driver. Diary, 1939–45, with emphasis on air raids and alerts and his activities as a firewatcher, with his daughters. IWM P121

734. *1939* RUMENS, J H, (male) of Walthamstow. Diary covers 1939–46, but only the 1939–41 sections refer to the London area. Recorded in some detail his experiences, including comments on ARP, rationing, firewatching and the bombing of London. He then joined the RAF, and became a clergyman after the war. IWM 87/8/1

735. *1939* SPEED, Florence, of Brixton and Streatham, artist and writer. Diary, 1939–44, 1946–8, 1948–64. A commercial artist pre-war, she joined the family clothing firm as a sales representative until its City premises were bombed in late 1940. Vivid descriptions of the Blitz, wartime difficulties, and her postwar experiences. IWM 86/45/2

736. *1939* STRANGE, *Miss* J C, of Worthing, Sussex, ARP worker. Most of the diaries relate to life in Worthing and her war work locally, but she frequently visited London and describes the devastation there after the air raids. IWM 96/13/2

737. *1939* THOMAS, *Miss* G, nurse. Diary covering her experiences at Highgate Hospital, Aug 1939–Jan 1943, and at Lewisham Hospital, Feb 1943–Aug 1945. Vivid entries on outbreak of war, the Blitz, V-weapon attacks, and her own and her patients' reactions. IWM 90/30/1

738. *1939* UPSHER, *Mrs* L M, of Camberwell. Photocopy of diary, Sept 1939–Sept 1945, with details of local air raids and alerts, bomb damage, and family matters. IWM 85/19/1

739. *1939* WAYTE, J W, Army officer (Lieutenant-Colonel, RAMC). War diary, Nov. 1939–April 1940 as officer commanding 189 Field Ambulance, in training at Barnet. Some personal material among notes on everyday army activities and the problems of setting up a new unit. Wellcome RAMC 1952/2

740. *1939* WEINER, *Miss* J, Citizen's Advice Bureau worker. Diary of her work in London, with comments on the air raids, her social life, the London Jewish community and German exiles. IWM 77/176/1 (R)

741. *1939* DE ZOETE, Beryl. Diary of writer's experiences in London at outbreak of Second World War; a friend of the orientalist Arthur Waley. Rutgers UL

742. *1940* ANON, (female) of London N6, temporary housekeeper. Diary, Feb–March 1940. M-O Diarist 5421

743. *1940* ANON, (female) of Crouch End, London N8, schoolteacher. Diary, 1940–42. M-O Diarist 5438

744. *1940* ANON, (male) of Muswell Hill, London N10, and Bourne, Cambs, bank clerk, and RAF (Flight Officer). Diary, 1940–56. M-O Diarist 5103

745. *1940* ANON, (female) of London N10. Diary, March 1940. M-O Diarist 5327.1

746. *1940* ANON, (male) of London N19. Diary, Aug 1940. M-O Diarist 5151

747. *1940* ANON, (female) of London NW1, and Orpington, Kent, office worker, housewife. Diary, 1940–5. M-O Diarist 5325

748. *1940* ANON, (male) of Mill Hill, London NW7, bookstall assistant. Diary, Feb 1940. M-O Diarist 5206

749. *1940* ANON, (female) of London NW11, and Harpenden, Herts. Diary, 1940. M-O Diarist 5388

750. *1940* ANON, (female) of London SE3, ambulance driver. Diary, 1940–1. M-O Diarist 5285

751. *1940* ANON, (female) of Brockley, London SE4, and Petworth, Sussex, housewife. Diary, 1940–4, 1947. M-O Diarist 5277

752. *1940* ANON, (male) of Deptford, London SE8, shopkeeper. Diary, 1940–2. M-O Diarist 5039.3

753. *1940* ANON, (male) of Plumstead, London SE18, engineer. Diary, 1940–2. M-O Diarist 5037

754. *1940* ANON, (male) of London SE26, Retired Electricity Board inspector. Diary, 1940–51. M-O Diarist 5098

755. *1940* ANON, (male) of London SW2, and Cirencester, Glos, office manager at Tea Propaganda Board. Diary, 1940–1. M-O Diarist 5006

756. *1940* ANON, (female) of London SW6, typist and full-time Mass Observer. Diary, Oct 1940. M-O Diarist 5257

757. *1940* ANON, (female) of London SW7, medical practitioner. Diary, Feb 1940. M-O Diarist 5386

758. *1940* ANON, (female) of London W5, housewife. Diary, 1940, 1942. M-O Diarist 5394

759. *1940* ANON, (female) of Maida Vale, London W9, housewife and voluntary worker. Diary, 1940–2. Extract (with pseudonym 'Mrs Crawford') in *Wartime Women* (ed D Sheridan 1990). M-O Diarist 5427

760. *1940* ANON, (male) of London W11, policeman. Diary, June–Aug 1940. M-O Diarist 5094

761. *1940* ANON, (male) of London WC1, and Geneva, lecturer. Diary, 1940, 1942. M-O Diarist 5082

762. *1940* ANON, (male) of Beckenham, Kent, and St Albans, Herts, schoolboy, later student. Diary, 1940–1. M-O Diarist 5091

763. *1940* ANON, (male) of Bromley, and Sidcup, Kent, commercial artist and gardener. Diary, 1940–2. M-O Diarist 5003

764. *1940* ANON, of Chelsea. Diary, 1940. Kensington LSL 940.548 EVE/AR/RS

765. *1940* ANON, (female) of Edgware, Middx, schoolgirl, student. Diary, June 1940, Feb 1941. M-O Diarist 5294

766. *1940* ANON, (female) of Harrow, Middx, civil servant. Diary, Aug–Dec 1940. Extract in *Wartime Women* (ed D Sheridan 1990). M-O Diarist 5244

767. *1940* ANON, (male) of Ickenham, Middx, HM Forces (Army). Diary, 1940–1. M-O Diarist 5130

768. *1940* ANON, (male) of Isleworth, Middx, Swindon, and Bournemouth, agricultural worker. Diary, 1940–1. M-O Diarist 5071

769. *1940* ANON, (female) of London, and Slough, Bucks, architect. Diary, 1940–50. M-O Diarist 5401

770. *1940* ANON, (female) of Ruislip, Middx. Diary, July 1940. M-O Diarist 5387

771. *1940* ANON, (male) of Twickenham, Middx, schoolteacher. Diary, 1940–3. M-O Diarist 5235

772. *1940* ANON, (male) of Wembley, Middx, commercial traveller. Diary, 1940–3. M-O Diarist 5150

773. *1940* ANON, (male) of Wembley, Middx, aircraft engineer. Diary, Jan–Feb 1940. M-O Diarist 5074

774. *1940* ANON, (male) of Woolwich, and Leeds, HM Forces (RAMC). Diary, 1940–2. M-O Diarist 5165

775. *1940* BACKHOUSE, F, (male) trainee journalist. Diary, Jan 1940–May 1941, kept while a trainee at the Canadian Press Agency. Describes his daily routine and spare time activities, covering the Battle of Britain, the Blitz and the resulting damage. IWM 90/16/1

776 *1940* BAWTREE, *Miss* V, of Sutton. Transcribed diary extracts, Aug 1940–Feb 1941, with detailed descriptions of Blitz raids over Surrey and London, their psychological effects on her, sheltering in the cellar, and make-shift Christmas celebrations. IWM 91/5/1

777. *1940* BRINTON-LEE, Diana, of West London, housewife, Women Drivers' Corps member. Diary, Aug 1940–May 1941. The writer and her husband lived near Wormwood Scrubs, but moved to a series of unsatisfactory lodgings in Buckinghamshire to escape the bombs. She continued to visit London frequently, and records reactions to wartime problems, air raids and bomb damage with clarity and humour. IWM P 178

778. *1940* CARPENTER, William H, of Caterham, businessman. Diary for 10 and 13 Sept 1940 detailing travel difficulties getting to and from his office in the City as a result of enemy action. LMA O/530/058

779. *1940* DEACON, *Mrs* A D, WRNS officer. Diary covering her war service including officer training at Greenwich. Air raids, alerts, VJ celebrations. IWM 89/17/1

780. *1940* FORD, Erica, of Ealing, canteen worker. Diary transcript, 1940–3, covering her domestic life, church involvement at St Peter's, Ealing, and war work in local fire service canteen. Ealing LHL

781. *1940* HODGSON, Vere, social worker in Notting Hill area. Diary, 1940–5. Extracts in her *Few Eggs and No Oranges* (1976). Kensington LSL Misc. 22466–72

782. *1940* JOHNSON, *Miss* D, of Edmonton, Deputy Head teacher. Diary, 23 May to 3 Oct 1940. She taught at Hazelbury Road School, Edmonton, and writes about air raids, casualties, damage and the effects of the raids on her family's life. Photocopy. IWM 89/14/1

783. *1940* KING, G W, of Sanderstead, law court shorthand writer. Diary, June 1940–Jan 1944, kept as a record for his son, a prisoner of war after Dunkirk. He notes the progress of war on all fronts, with his patriotic comments. Descibes how people coped with wartime disruption of all kinds. IWM 85/49/1

784. *1940* LEVERLAND, Ineke, of Carshalton Beeches, Dutch refugee. Mf diary, 1940–4. Mrs Leverland's husband managed the Philips plant in Croydon, making radios and parachutes for the Allied Forces. The diary covers the wearying effects of continual air-raids, family life in the Anderson shelter, low morale engendered by worry about family and friends in occupied Holland. A useful outsider's view of Britain at war. IWM PP/MCR/42

10-11-40 'I don't know which is better a
bad day or a bad night. Yesterday
it was one of those horrible raining cold
days, with low flying machine gunning
planes. The children went out for a short
and of course when the sirens went
did n't know what to do. After having
sat in the shops shelter they came home
by bus where I waited for them.
Hede is very nervous, kept on
going to the shelter while our
morpe. The night was quiet, while
today we had no warning at
all, the first time since this started.
But this evening with a bright
light of the growing moon the roar
of a thousand engines seem to be
bursting in my ears. It must be
a queer sight to see a person will
an orange coloured tin hat and
a loaded tea tray stepping across
the lawn. if a bomb would fall
the tea tray would be no more.
This morning the whole family
went to see E. T. who were
all here on their way to some other
place. They still seem to be afraid
of an invasion!

8. Ilse Leverland (**784**), a Dutch refugee, endures the Blitz in 1940 *(courtesy of the Imperial War Museum, Department of Documents)*

785. *1940* LOURDES, Sister, and MARY TERESA, Sister, nuns of the Convent of the Good Shepherd, Finchley. Diary, 'Summary of air raids in Finchley starting from August 1940', ending 1945. Much about convent life in general. Barnet ALS MS 16526

786. *1940* MARSLAND-GANDER, L, (male), radio correspondent of the *Daily Telegraph*. Diary July–Aug 1940 and Jan–Feb 1941, of his work in London and experiences on the Sussex coast. IWM 78/62/1

787. *1940* MOHAN, *Mr* and *Mrs* B P, clergyman, Vicar of St John's, Penge, and his wife. Diary 31 Aug 1940–5 Feb 1941, entitled 'Our Air Raid Book', about their precautions at the vicarage, air raid warnings in the area, bomb damage, casualties, and effects on their family. IWM 96/49/1

788. *1940* MORRIS, *Mrs* M, nurse. Transcript of nurse's diary; from May 1940–Feb 1943 she visited London frequently at weekends, describes air raids and conditions. From Feb 1943–May 1944 she nursed at the Brook Hospital, Woolwich, before overseas service. IWM 80/38/1

789. *1940* OAKMAN, *Miss* J M, of Chelsea, ARP warden and Food Office employee. Diary, 1940–5, with much on air raids, bomb incidents, daily life. IWM 91/20/1

790. *1940* POCOCK, Percy, of London, bank clerk. Diary, 1940 with occasional mention of firewatching duties and air raids. Sutton AS 55

791. *1940* REGAN, W B, of the Isle of Dogs, Beckenham and Catford, bricklayer and heavy duty rescue squad worker. Diary, with edited transcript, kept from Sept 1940 to Aug 1944, recording his service in the rescue squad on the Isle of Dogs during the Blitz. He was bombed out of his home, rehoused in Beckenham and Catford, worked as a bricklayer. Describes V1 raids, life on the Home Front and morale, rationing and entertainments. IWM 88/10/1

792. *1940* SHEPPERD, *Mrs* A, of Eltham, housewife. Diary covers the Blitz, Sept–Oct 1940, with descriptions of her family's daily routine during the air raids, her feelings, involvement with Methodist church. IWM 95/13/1

793. *1940* STEVENSON, *Mrs* M E, North London, secretary/typist. Diary, 1940–5, recording her office job in the City and evening munitions work, off duty entertainment and civilian conditions. IWM 86/56/1

794. *1940* THOMPSON, Joan, of Tottenham, schoolgirl, aged thirteen. Diary for the year 1940, of home and school life, local conditions, news and raids. IWM 90/16/1

795. *1940* TOUTAIN, Charlotte E, Nurse/switchboard operator with the Free French, writer had dual British/French nationality. Diary covers 1940–50, but she was in London only from 1940–4 and 1947–50. IWM Con Shelf, 90/5/1A

796. *1940* WARNER, *Miss* P, employee of Ministry of Home Security. Diary, Sept 1940–Feb 1942, with near daily entries describing her daily life at work, training as an emergency despatch rider, firewatching, helping at rest centre, air raids, Left wing politics, and London entertainments. IWM 95/14/1

797. *1940* WATERSON, Sidney, South African High Commissioner in London. Diary, 1940–2. Cape Town UL

798. *1940* WOODCOCK, S M S, (male) of Ladbroke Grove, ARP warden, and civil engineer. Diary, June 1940–Dec 1944 of his work as an air raid warden, with useful detail on ARP training, shelters and firewatching and conditions in general. He worked on the construction of the new Waterloo Bridge. IWM 87/36/1 (P)

799. *1941* ANON, (female) of London, HM Forces, (driver). Diary, Nov 1941. M-O Diarist 5403.1

800. *1941* ANON, (female) of East Ham, London E6, houseworker. Diary, 1941–3, 1947. M-O Diarist 5321

801. *1941* ANON, (male) of Southgate, London N14, accountant. Diary, 1941–2. M-O Diarist 5127

802. *1941* ANON, (female) of London SE9, office worker. Diary, 1941–2, 1944–7. M-O Diarist 5443

803. *1941* ANON, (female) of London SW3, housewife. Diary, 1941–2. M-O Diarist 5459

804. *1941* ANON, (female) of London SW5, Ulverston, Lancs, and Windermere, office worker in Fire Service and Home Office. Diary, 1941–2. M-O Diarist 5290

805. *1941* ANON, (male) of London SW12. Diary, 1941–2. M-O Diarist 5116

806. *1941* ANON, (female) of London SW19, secretary to Probation Officer. Diary, Jan 1941. M-O Diarist 5305

807. *1941* ANON, (male) of Acton, London W3, and Bury Port, Carm, HM Forces. Diary, Oct–Nov 1941. M-O Diarist 5112

808. *1941* ANON, (male) of London W5, chemist. Diary, Nov–Dec 1941, Feb 1942. M-O Diarist 5203

809. *1941* ANON, (male) of Belmont, Surrey, ARP worker and food packing manager. Diary, 1941–5. M-O Diarist 5004

810. *1941* ANON, (male) of Goodmayes, Essex, HM Forces (Army). Diary, Oct 1941–Jan 1942. M-O Diarist 5017

811. *1941* ANON, (male) of Hayes, Middx, factory laboratory worker. Diary, Oct 1941. M-O Diarist 5162

812. *1941* ANON, (male) of New Malden, Surrey, secretary of employees' association. Diary, 1941–5. M-O Diarist 5181

813. *1941* ANON, (female) of Purley, Surrey, and Belfast, tax inspector, and mother. Diary, 1941–4. M-O Diarist 5245

814. *1941* ANON, (male) of Sidcup, Kent, factory laboratory worker. Diary, 1941–2. M-O Diarist 5200

815. *1941* ANON, (female) of South Wallington, Surrey, housewife. Diary, Aug 1941. M-O Diarist 5327

816. *1941* ANON, (male) of West Drayton, Middx, office worker. Diary, 1941–3. M-O Diarist 5072

817. *1941* BOYCE, *Mrs* V I, housewife. Transcribed diary, July–Aug 1941, covers her voyage back to England from Canada to join her husband. She describes the effects of rationing on London and her enlistment in the WRNS. IWM 93/18/1

818. *1941* BRAHMS, Caryl, writer. Diary, May–Dec 1941, Jan–Feb 1942, July–Aug 1944, covering her literary work and duties as part-time ARP warden. IWM Con Shelf

819. *1941* CHANDLER, Ernest John, of Ealing, draper, Freemason. Diary, 1941, 1944–51. Domestic life, including meals, and business activities. Ealing LHL Acc 65

820. *1941* HOWARD, D, (female) of Kingston upon Thames, Surrey. Diary, 1941, of her firewatching duties in Upper Park Road. Kingston MHS KX177

821. *1941* JARVIS, H C M, (male), medical student, ARP warden. Diary, 1941, of life as a medical student and air raid warden. IWM 89/16/2(P)

822. *1941* KENT, D H, (male) of Adelaide Road, West Ealing. Diary, Jan–June 1941, recording times of every air raid alert, with general information about bombing throughout the country. IWM 99/9/1

823. *1941* QUINN, J E Gough, clergyman, Army officer (Chaplain). The diary covers his active service, 1940–3, but includes a month on leave in London in April–May 1941 with comments on morale, air raids, civilian conditions. IWM P247

824. *1941* RENTOUL, Alexander Laurence, RAAF (Senior Liaison Officer, Air Ministry). Diary kept while with the London Overseas HQ RAAF in the Air Ministry in London. Daily social activities, visits to RAF stations, aircraft factories and Bomber Command HQ. Australian WM PR89/171

825. *1941* RIDGWAY, F, (male), conscientious objector. Diary covers 1938–45 but London interest centres on Feb–June 1941 when he worked in London hospitals before training with the Friends' Ambulance Unit. IWM 67/347/1

826. *1941* TAYLOR, Reginald Charles, Vicar of St Bartholomew, Shepperton Road, Islington. Diary, Jan–April 1941. Covers everyday personal life and clerical duties, made more difficult by bombing and its aftermath. LMA P83/BAT/015

827. *1941* UTTIN, *Mrs* R E, of Wembley, housewife and war worker, mother of Miss D L Uttin, *qv*. Diary, 1941–5, with a few later entries for 1947–56. A record of air raids and alerts, bomb damage, firewatching, first aid classes, her directed war work at an aircraft components factory 1942–3, voluntary canteen and WVS work. Good detail on rationing, civilian conditions generally, V-weapons, and her attitude to Germany and war criminals. IWM 88/50/1

828. *1941* WILSON, June, student nurse. Diary, 1941–5, with long gaps between entries. Trained at Nightingale Training School, St Thomas's Hospital. LMA H1/ST/NTS/Y23/42

829. *1942* ANON, (female) of London NW6, schoolteacher and journalist. Diary, 1942. M-O Diarist 5384

830. *1942* ANON, (female) of London W2, office worker. Diary, 1942–3. M-O Diarist 5309

831. *1942* ANON, (male) of London, Salford and Edinburgh, HM Forces (articled clerk in Army). Diary, 1942–3. M-O Diarist 5177

832. *1942* ANON, (male) of Selsdon, Surrey, schoolteacher. Diary, 1942–5. M-O Diarist 5052

833. *1942* ANON, (male) of Sidcup, Kent, technical assistant, Ministry of Supply. Diary, Oct–Nov 1942. M-O Diarist 5169

834. *1942* ANON, (male) of West Drayton, Middx. Diary, March–Aug 1942. M-O Diarist 5127.1

835. *1942* BINNEY, Ralph Douglas, RN officer (Captain), Chief of Staff to Flag Officer, London. Diary, 1942–4. IWM 75/98/3

836. *1942* BREAKSPEAR, F B, (male), conscientious objector. Photocopy of a diary, covering Jan 1942–Nov 1943. The author was imprisoned in Brixton, Wandsworth and Wormwood Scrubs prisons for refusing a medical examination, and released on appeal to undertake full-time social work running a boys' club, and as an LCC Play Centre games leader. IWM 87/63/1

837 *1942* CHURCH-BLISS, *Miss* K, of Croydon, aircraft factory worker. Diary, Feb 1942–Nov 1944 (and transcript) of restaurant owner and friend ELSIE WHITEMAN, who left their business in Hampshire and moved to Croydon to help with war effort. Trained as lathe-turners, worked at Morrison's aircraft parts factory. Much on factory life, problems of women at work, industrial relations, morality, entertainment and general living conditions. IWM 91/34/1

838. *1942* LEE MICHELL, *Mrs* A, of Wellington, Somerset, WVS worker. Diary covers 1941–5, mostly concerns life in Somerset. However, in Jan 1942, and June–July 1944, during the V1 attacks, she visited London with the WVS and records her impressions. IWM 92/8/1(P)

839. *1942* PEAKE, Leonard G, RAAF (Flying Officer). Diary, 1942–5, of his wartime service at RAF bases in England. From Oct 1942–March 1944 he sometimes visited London on leave. IWM 99/64/1

840. *1942* SHARP, Evelyn, (female) journalist with Daily Herald. Diary, Aug 1942–May 1947. An edition is being prepared by Professor A.V. John of the University of Greenwich. Bodleian MS Eng. misc. d.668, e.634–6

841. *1942* STEEDS, A J, (male) of London, trainee actuary, then Army officer (Lieutenant). Transcribed diary, 1942–5, recording his wartime experiences. He was in London from Oct–Dec 1940 during the Blitz. IWM 99/31/1

842. *1943* ANON, (male) of Southgate, London N14, accountant's clerk. Diary, Nov 1943. M-O Diarist 5167

843. *1943* ANON, (female) of Forest Hill, London SE23, secretary. Diary, 1943–4. M-O Diarist 5429

844. *1943* ANON, (female) of Chelsea, London SW3, HM Forces (office worker for the military). Diary, March–May 1943. M-O Diarist 5417

845. *1943* ANON, (male) of London WC1, and New Forest, Hants, psychologist. Diary, March 1943. M-O Diarist 5085

846. *1943* ANON, (male) of London, and Cambridge, medical student. Diary, Jan–Sept 1943. M-O Diarist 5109

847. *1943* HOOPER, H F, RN officer (Lieutenant), Japanese translator. Writer trained as a translator and officer at Duchess House, West London, from Jan–Aug 1943 before service in the Far East, describing this period in his diary. IWM 95/5/1

848. *1943* O'RIORDAN, C T, RAAF officer. Diary, 1943, covering operations and recreation in between operations in London. Australian WM 3DRL/4164

849. *1943* UTTIN, *Miss* D, of Wembley, clerical assistant, daughter of *Mrs* R E Uttin, *qv*. Diary, Dec 1943–Aug 1945. Her work as assistant to the Harrow Youth Officer, leisure activities, local air raids. IWM 88/50/1

850. *1944* ANON, (male) of Enfield, Middx, woodworking machinist. Diary, Sept 1944–Feb 1945. M-O Diarist 5198

851. *1944* ANON, (female) of Kew, Surrey. Diary, Aug 1944. M-O Diarist 5357

852. *1944* ANON, (female) of London, clerk. Diary, April 1944. M-O Diarist 5428

853. *1944* ANON, (female) of Stanmore, Middx, shorthand typist. Diary, 1944–6. M-O Diarist 5303

854. *1944* COLMAN, G, of Newham. Diary, 1944–5, of bombing in London. Newham LSL

855. *1944* COSSINS, *Mrs* M, of Chepstow Place, W2, employee of British Museum. Diary, April 1944–April 1945, of life in London during the V-1 and V-2 attacks. Fear, danger, gradual acclimatisation. Her cultural interests, social life. IWM 92/25/1

856. *1944* HALL, W E, of Hackney, ARP messenger. Diary, 1944, of 'the new Blitz', the V-weapon attacks. His daily routine, mostly uneventful, but with occasional emergencies. Comments on the war news. Cartoons and sketches. Hackney AD M 4472

857. *1944* HOLMES, Kenneth, of Upper Holloway. Diary, June 1944–May 1945, aged sixteen, of flying bomb raids. Eye witness accounts of incidents, and from Sept 1944 he records V-2 attacks, including one that damaged his home. IWM P 129

858. *1944* HOME, Percy John, of Onslow Gardens, South Kensington. Diary entitled '1944: a London record', describing everyday life at the time of the flying bombs, with author's illustrations, newspaper cuttings, ephemera. Guildhall L MS 21, 599

859. *1944* JORY, C, (male), journalist, sub-editor of the News Chronicle. Diary, 1944, commenting on war news and events in London, including rocket hitting his block of flats while he was in bed, and his subsequent medical treatment. IWM 84/53/1

860. *1944* MASON, W E, Army officer (Lieutenant, Royal Signals). War diary, 1944–5, recording the actions of his Royal Signal Section. They include preparations for D-Day at Wanstead, and V-weapon raids over London in May–June 1944. IWM 89/13/1

861. *1944* SUMNER, E C, (male) of Leyton, auxiliary fireman. Diary, 1944, noting times of air raids, shifts worked as a fireman. IWM 98/22/1

862. *1944* TENBY-SMITH, Diana, student nurse. Diary, 1944–6, brief entries with long gaps. Trainee at Nightingale Training School, St Thomas's Hospital. LMA H1/ST/NTS/49

863. *1945* ANON, (female) of London, and Blackpool. Diary, May–Sept 1945. M-O Diarist 5243

864. *1945* PENN, Byron, of 372 Watford Way, Hendon. Diary of day to day life of an elderly couple in Hendon in the last year of the Second World War. Domestic activities, rationing. Barnet ALS MS 6111/2

865. *1945* STARKEY, F N E, of London. Diary covers 1945–9, London sections comprise Sept 1945–July 1947 during which time he entered a law firm and law school in the City before doing his National Service in the RAF, and Oct 1947–May 1948 when he was a clerk at the Air Ministry. IWM 94/10/1

866. *1946* HEELAS, *Mr*, of Norbiton, son of the Revd N Heelas, *qv*. Diary, 1946. Kingston MHS KX173/1/1/32

867. *1947* ANON, (male), House of Commons clerk. Diary, 1947. M-O G5321

868. *1947* HODGES, H Price, headmaster of small private school in Harrow. Diary, 1947–54. Access restricted until 2004. LMA ACC 1118

869. *1948* ANON, (female) of Morden, Surrey, housewife and voluntary worker. Diary, 1948–51. M-O Diarist 5474

870. *1950* HELPMANN, *Sir* Robert, ballet dancer. Diary, 1950–86, covering his work with the Sadlers Wells and Vic-Wells ballet companies, and the London theatrical world. Australian NL MS 7161

871. *1950* WHITE, *Sir* Thomas Walter, Australian High Commissioner in London. Diary, 1950–1, 1953–4, kept while serving in London. Australian NL MS 9184

872. *1951* FANNING, Joan, of Wellington, NZ, artist. Diary, 1951–63, covering study in London at the St Martin's School of Art and the Slade. M New Zealand MS 40 Access restricted

873. *1951* TODD, Leslie, of Surrey. Diary, 1924–67, mainly chronicling weekend excursions by bicycle, and annual holidays, but including a visit to the Festival of Britain in 1951. Extract in *The Observant Traveller* (ed R Gard 1989). Surrey HC 2830/1/3–32

874. *1952* PRITCHARD, Joan Edith, of Westminster. Diary, with household accounts, 1952–86. WCA Acc 1564

875. *1955* BENJAMIN, Joe, of London, community worker. Photocopy of diary covering *c.*1955–94. NE Lincs Archives 1044

876. *1955* FARMER, Kate, student at Hillcroft College, Surbiton. Diary, 1955, of a mature student. Kingston MHS KX357

877. *1957* LAKE, Larry, London liaison officer for Australian National Library. Diary, 1957–8, kept while working in London. Australian NL MS 8324

878. *1960* MOTTRAM, Eric, poet and academic at King's College, London. Diary 1960–93 covers his London life, with daily entries for activities, reading and listening. His earlier diaries (1951 on) do not deal with London. KCL Mottram 1/1/6–39

879. *1960* TENCH, Georgiana, of Wandsworth. Diary, 1960–3, while living with her daughter in Wandsworth. Warwick MRC MSS 255

880. *1963* BALFOUR, Donald and Louise, of Sydney, Australia. Diary, 1963 and 1968, of two voyages from Australia to England, with stays in London in the summer of each year. Australian NL MS 1010

881. *1971* CARTER, Sharon, of Ealing, schoolgirl. This and **882, 883** were kept by schoolchildren on Sunday, 25 April 1971 (Census Day) as part of a school project. Very detailed accounts of the full day's events at home. Ealing LHL Acc 41

882. *1971* CHOHAN, Navtej, of Ealing, schoolboy. Census day diary, 1971. Ealing LHL Acc 41

883. *1971* WONG, Diane, of Ealing, schoolgirl. Census day diary, 1971. Ealing LHL Acc 41

INDEX OF UNPUBLISHED
DIARISTS

The references are to item number.

SUBJECT INDEX TO
UNPUBLISHED DIARIES

The references are to item number.

THE SELECT BIBLIOGRAPHY OF
PUBLISHED DIARIES

In compiling the foregoing checklist of unpublished diaries I found numerous references to published London diaries. Many of them are very well-known, like the wonderful edition of the diary of Samuel Pepys by Robert Latham and William Matthews (Bell & Hyman, 1970–83), in nine volumes, with a companion volume and a full index, an exemplary work of scholarship to complement a wonderfully full and uninhibited journal of life in London in the 1660s. Other personal favourites of mine include William Tayler, a footman writing in 1837, and Ernest Baker, a schoolboy in 1881–82. I have therefore complemented the checklist with a bibliography of published editions. The field is so large, however, that the bibliography should not be regarded as comprehensive. Nevertheless, I hope that it will prove useful in conjunction with the unpublished sources. The bibliography is arranged by chronological order of diary starting date, with brief sections at first for general diary bibliographies, and for compilation volumes. Where more than one edition of a diary exists I have listed the most recent version. There is an index of authors and editors, but no subject index, which could only be so rudimentary as to be unhelpful.

Published diaries provide a most valuable quarry, though the editing process inevitably puts the user at one remove from the original. The high standards of much modern editing, giving clear indications of what has been omitted and how the material has been approached editorially, make this less of a problem than it once was. Editors of old, especially if they were piously presenting the diary of a great man to a respectful public, could be ruthlessly selective. The resulting edition can be oddly distorted and misleading and it is usually advisable to see the original, if still in existence. Those who edit their own diaries for publication are of course free to omit – or add – at will. As they frequently do.

SELECT BIBLIOGRAPHY OF
PUBLISHED LONDON DIARIES

General bibliographies

1. BATTS, JOHN STUART. British manuscript diaries of the 19th century: an annotated listing. Fontwell, Sussex: Centaur P, 1976. xi, 345pp.

2. CLINE, CHERYL. Women's diaries, journals and letters: an annotated bibliography. New York: Garland, 1989. xxxviii, 716pp.

3. COX, EDWARD GODFREY. A reference guide to the history of travel. Vol. 3, Great Britain. Seattle, Wa.: Washington UP, 1949. xiii, 732pp. [London section pp.234–91. Some London diaries in separate section 'Letters, diaries, memoirs'.]

4. HANDLEY, C S. An annotated bibliography of diaries printed in English. 3rd edn. Whitley Bay: Hanover P, 2002. 8 vols.

5. HAVLICE, PATRICIA PATE. And so to bed: a bibliography of diaries published in English. Metuchen, N J: Scarecrow P, 1987. viii, 698pp.

6. HUFF, CYNTHIA ANNE. British women's diaries: a descriptive bibliography of 19th century women's manuscript diaries. New York: AMS Press, 1985. xxxvi, 139pp.

7. KANNER, BARBARA. Women in English social history, 1800–1914: a guide to research. New York: Garland, 1987–90. 3 vols. [Contains bibliography of British women diarists.]

8. LINDEMAN, R, and others. Reisverslagen van Noordnederlanders... een chronologische lijst. Haarlem: Stichting Egodocument, 1994. 218pp.

9. MATTHEWS, WILLIAM. British diaries: an annotated bibliography of British diaries written between 1442 and 1942. Berkeley, Calif.: U California P, 1950. xxxiv, 339pp.

10. MATTHEWS, WILLIAM. American diaries in manuscript, 1580–1954. Athens, Ga: U Georgia P, 1974. xvi, 176pp. [Includes many of London relevance.]

Anthologies of diaries

11. BAGLEY, J J *(ed.)*. Lancashire diarists: three centuries of Lancashire lives. Phillimore, 1975. 210pp., illus. [Includes Richard Kay (doctor, at Guys 1743–44) and Miss Ireland Greene, in London for 1748–49 season.]

12. BLYTHE, RONALD *(ed.)*. The Penguin book of diaries. Penguin, 1991. ix, 364pp.

13. BLYTHE, RONALD *(ed.)*. Private words: letters and diaries from the Second World War. Viking, 1991. 310pp. [Includes some London items.]

14. BRETT, SIMON *(ed.)*. The Faber book of diaries. Faber, 1987. xii, 498pp.

15. CHARLES LETTS and CO. Letts keep a diary: catalogue of exhibition at the Mall Galleries, Sept.–Oct. 1987, on the history of diary-keeping in Great Britain from the 16th to the 20th century, in commemoration of 175 years of Letts. Letts, 1987. 82pp., illus.

16. CREATON, HEATHER. Victorian diaries: the everyday lives of Victorian men and women. Mitchell Beazley, 2001. 144pp., illus. [Extracts from diaries of: Leonard Wyon 1835–64 (checklist of unpublished diaries no. **373**); Maria Cust,1856–58 (**382**); John Pritt Harley, 1858 (**397**); Joseph Hékékyan, 1862 (**244**); Peter King, 1885; nurses from St Thomas's Hospital, 1896; James Woodroffe, 1892–95; Andrew Tait, 1893–94 (**539**).]

17. FOTHERGILL, ROBERT ANTONY. Private chronicles: a study of English diaries. Oxford: OUP, 1974. 214pp., illus.

18. NATIONAL BOOK LEAGUE. London's diaries from Samuel Pepys to Harold Nicolson. The League, 1970. 23pp.

19. PONSONBY, ARTHUR. English diaries: a review of English diaries from the 16th to the 20th century with an introduction on diary writing. Methuen, 1923. viii, 447pp.

20. PONSONBY, ARTHUR. More English diaries. Methuen, 1927. 250pp.

21. SCHIMANSKI, STEFAN K, and TREECE, HENRY *(eds.)*. Leaves in the storm: a book of diaries. Lindsay Drummond, 1947. 299pp.

22. TAYLOR, IRENE, and TAYLOR, ALAN *(eds.)*. The assassin's cloak: an anthology of the world's greatest diarists. Edinburgh: Canongate, 2000. xix, 686pp. [With many of London interest.]

Published diaries in chronological order of start date

23. *1544* SMITH, THOMAS *(ed.)*. Vitae quorundam eruditissimorum et illustrium virorum. Mortier, 1707. Varied pagn. [Includes family diary of SIR PETER YOUNG, 1544–1608.]

24. *1550* MACHYN, HENRY. The diary of Henry Machyn... from AD 1550 to AD 1563, *ed.*. J G Nichols. (Camden Soc. Pubns., 42). The society, 1848. xxxii, 464pp., illus.

25. *1552* FORMAN, SIMON. The autobiography and personal diary from 1552–1602, *ed.* J O Halliwell. Privately printed 1849. iv, 32pp.

26. *1562* MAGNO, ALESSANDRO. The London journal of Alessandro Magno, 1562, *ed.* C M Barron and others. *London Jour.,* IX (1983) 136–52.

27. *1577* DEE, JOHN.The diaries of John Dee, *ed.* E Fenton. Charlbury, Oxon: Day Books, 1998. xi, 369pp. [1577–1600.]

28. *1592* RYE, W B (*ed.*). England as seen by foreigners in the days of Elizabeth and James I: comprising translations of the journals of the two DUKES OF WIRTEMBERG in 1592 and 1610, with extracts from the travels of foreign princes and others. J R Smith, 1865. cxxxii, 300pp., illus.

29. *1597* VALDSTEJNA, ZDENEK BRTNICKYZ, *Baron.* The diary of BARON WALDSTEIN, a traveller in Elizabethan England, *transl.* G W Groos. Thames & Hudson, 1981. 184pp., illus. [1597–1603.]

30. *1599* PLATTER, THOMAS. Journals of two travellers in Elizabethan and early Stuart England: Thomas Platter and HORATIO BUSINO, *ed.* P Razzell. Caliban, 1995. 193pp., illus.

31. *1602* MANNINGHAM, JOHN. The diary of John Manningham of the Middle Temple, 1602–1603, *ed..* R P Sorlien. Hanover, N H: Rhode Island Univ., 1976. xi, 467pp.

32. *1617* YOUNG, W (*ed.*). The history of Dulwich College, with a life of the founder, EDWARD ALLEYN, and his diary, 1617–22. Bumpus, 1889. 2 vols., illus.

33. *1620* EVELYN, JOHN. The diary of John Evelyn, *ed.* E S De Beer. Oxford: OUP, 1959. 1307pp. [Covers 1620 to 1706.]

34. *1629* BOOTH, ABRAHAM. Some royal and other great houses in England: extracts from the journal of Abraham Booth, *ed.* H J Louw. *Archit. Hist.,* XXVII (1984) 503–9.

35. *1629* BOOTH, ABRAHAM. Een dienaer der Oost-Indische compagnie te Londen in 1629: journael van Abram Booth en zijn descriptie van Engelandt, *ed.* A Merens. The Hague: Stols, 1942. 275pp., illus.

36. *1635* HOOKE, ROBERT. The diaries of Robert Hooke, the Leonardo of London, 1635–1703, *ed.* R Nichols. Lewes, Sussex: Book Guild, 1994. 185pp., illus.

37. *1635* GREENE, JOHN. John Greene's diary, 1635–59, *ed.* E.M. Symonds. *EHR,* XLII (1928) 385–94; 598–604; XLIII (1929) 106–17. [Later Recorder of London. His social and student life at Lincoln's Inn.]

38. *1644* DAWES, *Sir* THOMAS. The diary of Sir Thomas Dawes, 1644. *Surrey Archeol. Coll.,* XXXVII (1926) 1–36. [Owner of Putney Park estate.]

39. *1651* HUYGENS, LODEWIJCK. The English journal, 1651–52, *ed.* A G H Bachrach and R G Collmer. (Sir Thomas Browne Inst. Pubns., n.s 1). Leiden: Leiden Univ., 1982 . x, 319pp., illus. [Huygens came to London with Dutch embassy in 1651.]

40. *1655* VINCENT, THOMAS. The diary of Thomas Vincent, undermaster of Westminster School, 1655, *ed.* J B Whitmore. *Bodleian Lib. Record,* V (1956) 308–11.

41. *1658* BENHAM, W GURNEY *(ed.)*. A great Essex lawyer's diary. *Essex Rev.*, XXXI no. 123 (1922) 160–73; no. 124 (1922) 179–94. [SIR JOHN ARCHER.]

42. *1660* PEPYS, SAMUEL. The diary, 1660–69, *ed.* R Latham and W Matthews. Bell, 1970–83. 11 vols. [Vol. 10 is a Companion, vol. 11 the index.]

43. *1661* BRODIE, ALEXANDER. The diary of Alexander Brodie of Brodie, *ed.* D Laing. Aberdeen: Spalding Club, 1863. 560pp. [In London for ten months in 1661.]

44. *1661* SCHELLINK, WILLIAM. The journal of William Schellink's travels in England, 1661–63, *ed.* M Exwood and H L Lehmann. (Camden 5th ser., 1). Royal Hist. Soc., 1993. 196pp.

45. *1666* MILWARD, JOHN. The diary of John Milward Esq., MP for Derbyshire, September 1666 – May 1668, *ed.* C. Robbins. CUP,1938. 349pp.

46. *1666* WADE, JOHN. Leaves from a 17th century parson, *ed.* G Huelin. *Church Quart. Rev.*, CLIX (1958) 246–55. [John Wade of Hammersmith.]

47. *1671* BOYS, JEFFREY. The diary of Jeffrey Boys of Gray's Inn, 1671, *ed.* G J Gray. *Notes and Queries*, CLIX (1930) 452–56.

48. *1671* FREKE, ELIZABETH. Mrs Elizabeth Freke: her diary, 1671–1714, *ed.* M Carbery. Cork: Guy, 1913. 43pp.

49. *1680* LEVER, JAMES. A London citizen's diary in the 17th and 18th centuries, *c*.1680–1746, *ed.* A A L Wallis. *Reliquary*, n.s. III (1889) 90–8; IV (1890) 135–41; V (1891) 13–20.

50. *1684* SWEDBERG, JESPER. Swedbergs lefwernes beskrifning, *ed.* G Wetterberg. Lund: Gleerup, 1941. 722pp. [Swedish clergyman's travels, including diary of a London visit in 1684.]

51. *1693* MANNERFELT, CARL OTTO. Mannerfeltska släktboken. Borås, 1918. 249pp. [Contains diary of a Swedish naval officer on a visit to London in 1693. In Swedish.]

52. *1702* NICOLSON, WILLIAM. The London diaries of William Nicolson, bishop of Carlisle, 1702–18, *ed.* C Jones and G Holmes. Oxford: Clarendon P, 1985. xxi, 772pp.

53. *1710* BREDBERG, SVEN. Greifswald – Wittenberg – Leiden – Londen: Västgötamagistern Sven Bregbergs resedagbok, 1708–10, *ed.* H Sandblad. (Acta Bibliotheca Scarensis, 3). Skara: Stifts-o.Landsbibl.1982. 135pp. [Swedish travel diary, with English summary.]

54. *1710* UFFENBACH, ZACHARIAS CONRAD von. London in 1710, *ed.* W H Quarrell and M M Mare. Faber, 1934. 194pp.

55. *1712* BAKER, JOHN. The diary of John Baker, *ed.* P C Yorke: a record of family history and society in England (mostly in Sussex and London) and the Leeward Islands. Hutchinson, 1931. xvii, 517pp. [1712–79.]

56. *1715* RYDER, DUDLEY. The diary of Dudley Ryder, 1715–16, *ed.* W Matthews. Methuen, 1939. xi, 407pp., illus. [Law student.]

57. *1717* BYRD, WILLIAM. William Byrd of Virginia: the London diary, 1717–21, *ed.* L B Wright and M Tinling. New York: OUP, 1958. vi, 647pp.

58. *1721* SAVILLE, GERTRUDE. Secret comment: the diaries of Gertrude Saville, 1721–57, *ed.* A Saville. (Thoroton Soc. Record ser., 41). The Society, 1997. xvi, 390pp. [Often in London.]

59. *1731* WILSON, THOMAS. The diaries of Thomas Wilson, D.D., 1731–37, and 1750, *ed.*. C L S Linnell. SPCK, 1964. ix, 264pp., illus. [Whig clergyman.]

60. *1737* OLDYS, WILLIAM. A literary antiquary: memoir of William Oldys, together with his diary. Spottiswoode, 1862. 116pp. [Diary extracts, pp.1–29, cover 1737–39.]

61. *1749* DODINGTON, GEORGE BUBB, *Baron Melcombe*. The diary of the late George Bubb Dodington... 1749 to 1761... Hunt & Clarke, 1828. vi, 279pp., illus.

62. *1749* GIBBONS, THOMAS. Dr Thomas Gibbons' diary, ed. W H Summers. *Congregational Hist. Soc. Trans.,* I (1901–04) 312–29, 380–97; II (1905–06) 22–38; IV (1909–10) 29–36. [Diary extracts, 1749–85. Minister of the Independent Church, Haberdashers' Hall.]

63. *1758* FERRNER, BENGT. Resa i Europa: en astronom, industrispion och teaterhabitu, genom Danmark...England...och Italien, 1758–62, *ed.* S G Lindberg. (Lychnos Bibliotek, 14). Uppsala: Almqvist & Wiksell, 1956. lxxxvii, 572pp. [Swedish traveller.]

64. *1761* KIELMANSEGGE, FRIEDRICH, *Graf von*. Diary of a journey to England in 1761–62. Longmans, 1902. vi, 286, 40pp., illus.

65. *1762* BOSWELL, JAMES. Boswell's London journal, 1762–63, *ed.* F A Pottle. Heinemann, 1950. xii, 370pp., illus.

66. 1762 RICHARDSON, A E. ROBERT MYLNE, architect and engineer. Batsford, 1955. 220pp., illus. [He built Blackfriars Bridge. Contains extracts from Mylne's diaries, 1762–1810, pp.57–220.]

67. *1763* LALANDE, JOSEPH J LE F DE. Journal d'un voyage en Angleterre, 1763, avec une introduction par H Monod-Cassidy. (Studies on Voltaire and the 18th century, 184).Oxford: Taylor Inst. .1980. 116pp., illus.

68. *1764* BRIETZCKE, CHARLES. Charles Brietzcke's diary (1764). *Notes and Queries,* CCVI (1961) 9–14, 61–63, 83–86, 144–47, 191–93, 210–14, 258–62, 302–07, 335–39, 391–95, 433–44, 452–61.

69. *1764* MAWHOOD, WILLIAM. The Mawhood diary: selections from the diary notebooks of William Mawhood, woollen-draper of London, for the years 1764–90, *ed.* E E Reynolds. (Catholic Record Soc. Pubns., 50.) The society, 1956. 291pp.

70. *1765* BINYON, EDWARD. Diary of a London Quaker apprentice, 1765–68. *Friends' Hist. Soc. Jour.,* XXI (1924) 45–52.

71. *1767* NEVILLE, SYLAS. The diary of Sylas Neville, 1767–88, *ed.* B Cozens-Hardy. Oxford: OUP, 1950. 357pp. [Frequently in London.]

72. *1768* BURNEY, FANNY. The early journals and letters of Fanny Burney, *ed.* L E Troide. Vols. 1–3, 1768–79. Oxford: OUP, 1994. 3 vols. [1768–1840.]

73. *1770* LICHTENBERG, GEORG CHRISTOPH, *the elder.* Lichtenberg's visits to England (1770 and 1774–5) as described in his letters and diaries, *ed.* M M Mare and W H Quarrell. Oxford: Clarendon P, 1938. xxiv, 130pp. [Much on London.]

74. *1771* PEEL, ALBERT. The diary of a deacon at White Row chapel, Spitalfields. *Congregational Hist. Soc. Trans.,* XV (1944–8) 177–85. [1771–92.]

75. *1772* LEWIN, T H *(ed.).* The Lewin letters. Privately printed 1909. 2 vols. [Vol. 1 contains extracts from the private diary, 1772–1829, of RICHARD LEWIN, a Trinity House officer living in Eltham.]

76. *1773* BEATTIE, JAMES. James Beattie's London diary, 1773, *ed.* R S Walker. Aberdeen Univ. Studies, 122). Aberdeen: Aberdeen U.P.1946. 145pp., illus.

77. *1774* YEOMAN, JOHN. The diary of the visits of John Yeoman to London in 1774 and 1777, *ed.* M Yearsley. Watts, 1935. v, 55pp., illus.

78. *1775* CAMPBELL, THOMAS. Dr Campbell's diary of a visit to England in 1775, *ed.* J L Clifford. Cambridge: CUP, 1947. xv, 147pp., illus.

79. *1775* CURWEN, SAMUEL. The journal of Samuel Curwen, loyalist, *ed.* A Oliver. Cambridge, Mass.: Harvard UP, for Essex Inst., 1972. 2 vols. [American loyalist in London.]

80. *1775* FISHER, JABEZ NAUD. An American Quaker in the British Isles: the travel journals of Jabez Naud Fisher, 1775–79, *ed.* K Morgan. Oxford: British Academy, for OUP, 1992. xi, 356pp.

81. *1777* ALLEN, JOHN. Leaves from the past: the diary of John Allen, 1777, *ed.* C Y Sturge. Simpkin, 1905. 96pp. [Wapping brewer.]

82. *1781* GREVILLE, ROBERT FULKE. The diaries of Robert Fulke Greville, equerry to HM King George III, *ed.* F M Bladon. Bodley Head, 1930. 375pp. [1781–94.]

83. *1783* BERRY, MARY. Extracts of the journals and correspondence from the year 1783 to 1852, *ed.* Lady T Lewis. 2nd edn. Longmans Green, 1866. 3 vols. [Refers to Walpole and Strawberry Hill.]

84. *1784* WINDHAM, WILLIAM. The diary of William Windham, 1784–1810, *ed.* Mrs H Baring. Longmans, 1866. 540pp. [1784–1810. Politician.]

85. *1786* LA ROCHE, SOPHIE von. Sophie in London, 1786: being the diary of Sophie von La Roche, transl. C Williams. Cape, 1933. 307pp.

86. *1786* SWAN, WILLIAM THOMAS, and SWAN, WILLIAM. The journals of two poor dissenters, 1786–1880. Routledge, 1970. xv, 102pp. [Labourers.]

87. *1786* ORIANI, BARNABA. Un viaggio in Europa nel 1786: diario di Barnaba Oriani, astronomo milanese, *ed.* A Mandrino and others. Florence: Olschki, 1994. 225pp., illus.

88. *1789* PONSONBY, VERE BRABAZON, *Earl of Bessborough (ed.)*. Lady Bessborough and her family circle. Murray, 1940. xx, 307pp. [Contains extracts from the social diary of HENRIETTA FRANCES, COUNTESS OF BESSBOROUGH, March–April 1789.]

89. *1790* MORRIS, GOUVERNEUR. A diary of the French Revolution, *ed.* B C Davenport. Harrap, 1939. 2 vols., illus. [Includes author's impressions of London when on US diplomatic mission, 1790–92.]

90. *1791* PORTER, AGNES. A governess in the age of Jane Austen: the journals and letters of Agnes Porter, *ed.* J Martin. Hambledon, 1998. 372pp., illus. [The journals cover 1790–1805 and include visits to London, the first in 1791.]

91. *1793* FARINGTON, JOSEPH. The diary of Joseph Farington, *ed.* K Garlick and A Macintyre. New Haven, Conn.: Paul Mellon Center, 1978–. Vol. 1 –. In progress. [Topographical artist, his diaries run from 1793–1821.]

92. *1793* CREEVEY, THOMAS. The Creevey papers: a selection from the correspondence and diaries of the late Thomas Creevey, MP, *ed.* Sir H Maxwell. Murray, 1904. 2 vols. [Anecdotes and London gossip, 1793–1838.]

93. *1795* MACRITCHIE, WILLIAM. Diary of a visit to London in 1795, notes by D Macritchie. *Antiquary,* XXXII (1896) 237–42, 270–75. [Clergyman. Full tour was published as *Diary of a Tour through Great Britain in 1795* (Elliot Stock, 1897).]

94. *1796* MACAULAY, GEORGE MACKENZIE. The war diary of a London Scot, 1796–7. Paisley: Gardner, 1916. 216pp. [Master of the Bowyers' Company.]

95. *1800* LAURIE, *Sir* PETER. The journal of Sir Peter Laurie. Costello, 1985. 153pp. [The diary covers 1800–59. He was Lord Mayor, 1832–33. Also Master of the Saddlers' Company and President of Bridewell and Bethlem Hospitals.]

96. *1803* SCHOPENHAUER, JOHANNA. A lady travels: the diaries of Johanna Schopenhauer, *ed.* R Michaelis-Jena and W Merson. Routledge, 1988. xv, 245pp., illus. [1803–05. London and environs, pp.134–245.]

97. *1808* CROKER, JOHN WILSON. The correspondence and diaries, *ed.* L J Jennings. Murray, 1884. 3 vols. [1801–57. Politician and essayist.]

98. *1808* HAYDON, BENJAMIN ROBERT. Neglected genius: the diaries of Benjamin Robert Haydon, 1808–46, *ed.* J Jolliffe. Hutchinson, 1990. xii, 260pp., illus. [Artist.]

99. *1809* ABU AL-HASSAN KHAN. A Persian at the court of King George, 1809–10: the journal of Mirza Abul Hassan Khan, *transl.* and *ed.* M Morris Cloake. Barrie & Jenkins, 1988. 318pp., illus. [Translation of *Hayratnamah-i sufara.*]

100. *1810* SIMOND, LOUIS. Journal of a tour and residence in Great Britain during 1810 and 1811. 2nd edn. Edinburgh: Constable, 1817. 2 vols. [Vol. 1, pp. 21–235 on London.]

101. *1811* BAILEY, JAMES BLAKE. The diary of a resurrectionist, 1811–12, and an account of the resurrection men in London. Sonnenschein, 1896. 184pp., illus.

102. *1811* ROBINSON, HENRY CRABB. Diary, reminiscences and correspondence, *ed.* T Sadler. Macmillan, 1869. 3 vols. [A selection of his theatrical entries was published as *The London Theatre 1811–66, ed.* E Brown (Soc. Theatre Research, 1966).]

103. *1813* BLAKE, *Mrs* WARRENNE *(ed.)*. Memoirs of a vanished generation. Lane, 1909. xxxviii, 308pp., illus. [Pp.5–56: extracts from the London social diary of JANE SOPHIA HOPE KNOX, 1813–19.]

104. *1814* FISCHER, J C. J C Fischer and his diary of industrial England, 1814–51, by W.O. Henderson. Cass, 1966. xvi, 184pp., illus. [With sections on London.]

105. *1818* MANTELL, GIDEON. The journal of Gideon Mantell, surgeon and geologist, 1818–52, *ed.* E C Curwen. Oxford: OUP, 1940. xii, 315pp.

106. *1818* MOORE, THOMAS. The journal of Thomas Moore, *ed.* W S Dowden and others. Assoc. UP, 1983–91. 6 vols. [Poet. Diaries cover 1818–47, much on London.]

107. *1819* NEUMANN, PHILIPP, *Freiherr von*. The diary...1819–50, *ed.* E B Chancellor. Philip Allan, 1928. 2 vols., illus. [Diplomat.]

108. *1819* RUSH, RICHARD. A residence at the Court of London. Century, 1987. xvii, 239pp. [American ambassador's diary, 1819–25. Originally pubd. 1833.]

109. *1819* WINSTON, JAMES. Drury Lane journal: selections from James Winston's diaries, 1819–27, *ed.* A L Nelson and G B Cross. Soc. Theatre Research, 1974. xv, 176pp., illus.

110. *1820* GREVILLE, CHARLES. The Greville diary, *ed.* P W Wilson. Heinemann, 1927. 2 vols., illus. [1820–60. Clerk to the Privy Council.]

111. *1821* ADAMS, PERCY W L *(ed.)*. A history of the Douglas family... Bedford: Sidney P, 1921. xxiii, 925pp. [Pp.545–48: extracts from the travel diary of HENRY DOUGLAS, 1821, including a visit to London.]

112. *1822* GREENWOOD, ANN MARIA. The diary of Anna Maria Greenwood, 1822–32, *ed.* D S Cooper. The editor, 1997. 183pp.

113. *1822* RICHARDSON, *Sir* BENJAMIN W. THOMAS SOPWITH: with excerpts from his diary... Longmans, 1891. xii, 400pp. [Pp.15–360: extracts from diary, 1822–79, of engineer with wide social and cultural interests.]

114. *1823* BAKER, *Mr.* A chronicle of the damned, *ed.* M Cheyney. Ramsey, Cambs.:Family Tree Mag., 1990. 50pp., illus. [Diary of a Mr Baker, of the death cells at Newgate 1823–24.]

115. *1823* FRY, W H P *(ed.).* Annals of the late MAJOR OLIVER FRY, RA. Lund Humphries, 1909. 104pp., illus. [Pp.42–81: extracts from his diary, 1823–60, including visits to London from Ireland.]

116. *1823* LEWIN, WILLIAM. The Lewin diary: a link with Rennie, *ed.* H W Dickinson. *Newcomen Soc. Trans.*, XIX (1938–9) 109–17. [Engineer, assistant to John Rennie. Diary covers 1823–27.]

117. *1823* NICHOLS, MARY ANNE. The diary of Mary Anne Nichols, 1823–34: a publisher's daughter in Hampstead, *ed.* J Pooley. *LAMAS Trans.*, XLIV (1993) 171–96.

118. *1823* TRANT, CLARISSA SANDFORD. The journal of Clarissa Trant, *ed.* C G Luard. John Lane, 1925. xxi, 335pp. [Society life in London, 1823–32.]

119. *1823* WHEATON, NATHANIEL SHELDON. Journal of a residence during several months in London. Hartford, Conn.: n.p.,1830. no.pag. [American clergyman's travel diary, 1823–24.]

120. *1824* FOX, MARIA. Memoirs of Maria Fox. Charles Gilpin, 1846. n.pag. [Includes extracts from her diary, 1824–43, with visits to London and Tottenham.]

121. *1824* WEETON, ELLEN. Miss Weeton's journal of a governess, 1807–25, *ed.* E Hall. Newton Abbot, Devon: David & Charles, 1969. 2 vols. [Pp.265–318, a visit to London, May–July 1824.]

122. *1825* GLADSTONE, WILLIAM EWART. The Gladstone diaries, *ed.* M R D Foot. Oxford: Clarendon P, 1968–94. 14 vols. [Statesman, Prime minister. Diaries cover 1825–96.]

123. *1825* SCOTT, *Sir* WALTER. The journal of Sir Walter Scott, *ed.* W E K Anderson. Edinburgh: Canongate, 1998. xlviii, 812pp. [1825–32. He frequently visited London.]

124. *1826* POCOCK, JOHN THOMAS. The diary of a London schoolboy, 1826–30, *ed.* M Holder and C A Gee. Camden Hist. Soc., 1980. xvii, 87pp., illus. [Family lived in Kilburn.]

125. *1826* TRISTAN, FLORA. The London journal of Flora Tristan, *ed.* J Hawkes. Virago, 1982. xlii, 306pp., illus. [Four visits between 1826–39.]

126. *1829* STEPHENS, WILLIAM R W *(ed.).* A memoir of the Rt Hon W P WOOD, BARON HATHERLEY. Bentley, 1883. 2 vols. [Vol. 1 contains extracts from Baron Hatherley's diary, 1828–29, covering his studies at Lincoln's Inn, and his social life.]

127. *1830* CHALMERS, ANNE. Letters and journals, *ed.* A W Blackie. Curwen P, 1923.,n.pag. [Lively 17 year old's account of year's visit to London with her father in 1830. Parliament, clergy, visits, social life and so on.]

128. *1830* POST, FREDERIC JAMES. Extracts from the diary and other manuscripts of the late F J Post, of Islington, with a memoir. Moyes, 1838. xx, 476pp. [A Quaker. The diary covers 1830–35.]

129. *1831* FOX, HENRY R.V., *Baron Holland*. The Holland House diaries, 1831–40, with extracts from the diary of Dr John Allen, *ed.* A D Kriegel. Routledge, 1977. lxiv, 513pp.

130. *1831* RAIKES, THOMAS. A portion of a journal kept ...from 1831 to 1847; comprising reminiscences of social and political life in London and Paris during that period. Longmans, 1856–58. 4 vols.

131. *1832* COLLIER, JOHN PAYNE. An old man's diary. Privately printed, 1871. 72pp. [Covers 1832–33. His social life and literary contacts.]

132. *1832* GREVILLE, HENRY WILLIAM. Leaves from the diary of Henry Greville, *ed.* Viscountess Enfield. Smith, Elder, 1883, 1884. 2 vols. [Man about town. 1832–72.]

133. *1832* VICTORIA, *Queen*. The girlhood of Queen Victoria: a selection from Her Majesty's diaries, 1832–40, *ed.* Viscount Esher. Murray, 1912. 2 vols.

134. *1833* MACREADY, WILLIAM CHARLES. The journal of William Charles Macready, *ed.* J C Trewin. Longmans, 1967. xxxiii, 315pp. [Actor. The diary covers 1833–51.]

135. *1833* TILT, JANE. A month in Hampstead: the journal of a visit March–April 1833. *Camden Hist. Rev.,* no.17 (1992) 9–12.

136. *1834* WESTREENEN VAN TIELLANDT, W H J, *Baron van*. Journal...van zijn reizen naar Londen, Cambridge en Oxford in de jaren 1834 en 1835, *ed.* D van Velden. The Hague: Rijksmuseum Meermanno-Westreenianum, 1972. 88pp., illus.

137. *1835* BUDGE, JANE [?]. A beloved mother, by her daughter, J B Harris, 1884. viii, 188pp. [Pp. 34–109: extracts from Quaker diary of HANNAH ALLEN, 1835–49. Life in Clapton and central London.]

138. *1836* CARPENTER, JAMES STRATTON. The 1836 London diary of James Stratton Carpenter MD, *ed.* T Reed Ferguson. Minerva, 1996. xiv, 108pp.

139. *1836* HALLIWELL-PHILLIPPS, HENRIETTA. A Victorian chronicle: the diary of Henrietta Halliwell-Phillipps, *ed.* M Spevack. New York: Olms, 1999. 370pp., illus. [London and the country.]

140. *1836* KINGSFORD, P W, *and* JONES, A (*eds.*). Down and out in Hertfordshire. Stevenage, Herts.: Hertfordshire Pubns., 1984. 187pp., illus. [Contains: The diary of BENJAMIN WOODCOCK, Master of the Barnet Union workhouse, 1836–38.]

141. *1836* NAJAF-KULI MIRZA, *Prince of Persia*. Journal of a residence in England ... *transl.* A Y Khayyat. Tyler, 1839. 2 vols. [Vol. 2, pp.17–163, covers his stay in London.]

142. *1837* ARMSTRONG, BENJAMIN JOHN. A Middlesex diary, *ed.* M Robbins. *LAMAS Trans.*, n.s. XI pt.2 (1954) 105–14. [Clergyman. Covers 1837.]

143. *1837* SULLY, THOMAS. Queen Victoria and Thomas Sully, *ed.* C B Barratt. Princeton, NJ: Princeton UP, 2000. 224pp., illus. [Diary of American artist's visit to England, 1837–38.]

144. *1837* TAYLER, WILLIAM. Diary of William Tayler, footman, 1837, *ed.* D Wise and A Cox-Johnson. (St Marylebone Soc. Pubns., 7). The society, 1987. 63pp.

145. *1833* JENKINSON, JOSEPH. The diary of Joseph Jenkinson of Dronfield, 1833–43, *ed.* K M Battye. (Derbys. Record Soc. Occas. Papers, 7). The society, 1987. 95pp. [Worked at hat factory in Southwark, 1839–43. Anti-Corn Law League and Chartism.]

146. *1840* DOYLE, RICHARD. Richard Doyle's journal, 1840, *ed.* C Wheeler. Edinburgh: Bartholomew, with British Museum Pubns., 1980. xvii, 156pp.

147. *1840* RICE, CHARLES. Tavern singing in early Victorian London: the diaries of Charles Rice for 1840 and 1850, *ed.* L Senelick. Soc. Theatre Research, 1997. xxxiv, 265pp., illus.

148. *1840* BAGER, JOHAN PETER. Impressions of London from the later summer of 1840: the thoughts and experiences of a Swedish gentleman, *ed.* L Hansen. Whitby, N. Yorks.: IKFoundation, 2001. 160pp., illus.

149. *1844* BROWN, FORD MADOX. The diary, *ed.* V Surtees. New Haven, Conn.: Paul Mellon Center, 1981. xv, 237pp. illus. [Artist. Covers 1844–56.]

150. *1845* STEELE, EDWARD. Edward Steele: the journal of a Victorian, *ed.* A Hutchings. Charlotte James Pubrs., 1982. 223pp., illus. [1845–99, mainly London.]

151. *1845* WAKEFIELD, EDWARD JERNINGHAM. The London journal of Edward Jerningham Wakefield, 1845–54 *ed.* J Stevens. Wellington, NZ: Alexander Turnbull Lib., 1972. xv, 179pp., illus.

152. *1846* MELVILLE, GANSEVOORT. Gansevoort Melville's 1846 London journal and letters from England, 1845, *ed.* H Parker. New York: New York Public Lib., 1966. 74pp., illus.

153. *1849* LEEVES, EDWARD. Leaves from a Victorian diary. Alison P, Secker, 1985. vii, 192pp.

154. *1849* MELVILLE, HERMAN. Journal of a visit to London and the continent, 1849–50, *ed.* E M Metcalf. Cohen, 1949. xvii, 172pp., illus.

155. *1851* BOYCE, GEORGE PRICE. The diaries of George Price Boyce, *ed.* V Surtees. Norwich: Real World, 1980. 127pp., illus. [Artist. Diaries cover 1851–75. Originally pubd. 1941.]

156. *1851* MORLEY, HENRY. Journal of a London playgoer from 1851 to 1866. Routledge, 1866. 384pp.

157. *1854* ROBERTS, NATHANIEL. Coomb Farm diary, 1854, *ed.* B Tunstall. *Greenwich and Lewisham Antiq. Soc. Trans.*, IV (1936–53) 207–35.

158. *1854* CULLWICK, HANNAH. The diaries of Hannah Cullwick, Victorian maidservant, *ed.* L Stanley. Virago, 1984. viii, 327pp., illus. [1854–73. Secret wife of Arthur Munby, *qv.*]

159. *1857* BAIN, J S. A bookseller looks back: the story of the Bains. Macmillan, 1940. xv, 304pp., illus. [Contains the diary of Louisa Bain, 1857–83.]

160. *1857* MORAN, BENJAMIN. The journal of Benjamin Moran, 1857–65, *ed.* S A Wallace and F E Gillespie. Chicago: Chicago U.P.1948. 2 vols. [Assistant Secretary at the American Legation in London.]

161. *1858* HARVEY, EDWARD. A postman's round, 1858–61: selected extracts from the diary of Edward Harvey, *ed.* R Storey. Coventry, Warwicks.: Warwick Univ. Lib., 1982. 52pp. [Letter-carrier in East London.]

162. *1859* HARDMAN, *Sir* WILLIAM. A mid-Victorian Pepys: Sir William Hardman, *ed.* S M Ellis. Palmer, 1923, 1925. The Hardman papers: a further selection, 1865–68, *ed.* S M Ellis. Constable, 1930. 3 vols. [Extracts from Hardman's social diary, 1859–68.]

163. *1859* MUNBY, ARTHUR F. Munby: man of two worlds: the life and diaries of Arthur F Munby, 1828–1910. Murray, 1972. ix, 461pp., illus. [1859–98. Writer, civil servant. Secretly married to Hannah Cullwick, *qv.*]

164. *1860* BUXTON, ELLEN. Ellen Buxton's journal, 1860–64, *ed.* E R C Creighton. Bles, 1967. 96pp., illus.[Family lived at Leytonstone, frequently visited central London.]

165. *1861* HALDAR, RAKHAL DAS. The English diary of an Indian student. Dacca: Asutosh Lib., 1903).112pp. [Diary of a Bengali student at University College, 1861–62.]

166. *1863* ALLINGHAM, WILLIAM. William Allingham's diary, 1847–89, *ed.* G Grigson. Fontwell, Sussex: Centaur, 1967. xii, 404pp., illus. [Poet. In London from 1863.]

167. *1863* WILTON, FREDERICK C. The Britannia diaries, 1863–75: selections from the diaries of F C Wilton, *ed.* J Davis. Soc. Theatre Research, 1992. 263pp., illus.

168. *1866* RAPPE, EMMY CAROLINA. Emmy Carolina Rappe i London, 1866–67, *ed.* S G Sjoberg. (Sydsvenska Medicinhistoriska Sallskapets Arsskrift, Suppl., 10). Lund: the Univ., 1988. 96pp. [Describes London hospitals.]

169. *1872* KINWUN, MINGYI *('Minister').* Kinwun Mingyi's London diary, *ed.* U Gaung. Rangoon: Supdt. Govt. Printing & Stationery, 1927. n.pag. [Burmese ambassador.]

170. *1873* SWINTON, G C. Two generations. Macmillan, 1940. xxvii, 308pp. [Contains: Vestals and vestries: diary, 1873–77, of FLORENCE ALICE SITWELL's country life at Renishaw and visits to London, pp.147–308.]

171. *1873* WEBB, BEATRICE. The diary of Beatrice Webb, 1872–1943, *ed.* N and J MacKenzie. Virago, for LSE, 1982–85. 4 vols. [Social reformer.]

172. *1874* MCCREE, GEORGE WILSON. George Wilson McCree: his life and his work, with extracts from his journals, *ed.* C W McCree. Clarke, 1893. 212pp., illus. [Pastor of Borough Road Baptist chapel, 1874–92.]

173. *1877* DUFF, *Sir* MOUNTSTUART E G. A Victorian diarist at York House: Sir Mountstuart Elphinstone Grant Duff, 1877–96, *ed.* D H Simpson. (Twickenham Local Hist. Soc. Papers, 1). The Soc.1965. 16pp.

174. *1879* COBDEN-SANDERSON, THOMAS JAMES. The journals of Thomas James Cobden-Sanderson, 1879–1922. The author, 1926. 2 vols. [Bookbinder, of Goodyers, Brent Street Hendon, 1885–92. Repubd. New York: Franklin, 1969.]

175. *1880* HAMILTON, *Sir* EDWARD WALTER. Diary of Sir Edward Walter Hamilton, *ed.* D W R Bahlman: 1880–85. Clarendon P, 1972. 1885–1906: Hull: Hull UP, 1993. 3 vols., illus. [Assistant Private Secretary to Gladstone.]

176. *1881* BAKER, ERNEST. A Victorian schoolboy in London: the diary of Ernest Baker, 1881–82. Geffrye Museum, 1990. 94pp., illus. [Attended Dr Julius Klein's crammer at 110 Cannon Street.]

177. *1882* COMPTON, CHARLES. The diary of Charles Compton, artist and civil servant (1828–84), *ed.* E H Turner. Ilfracombe, Devon: Stockwell, 1980. 132pp., illus. [Diary covers 1882. He worked at Woolwich Dockyard and lived nearby.]

178. *1884* PENNELL, ELIZABETH ROBINS. The early London journals of Elizabeth Robins Pennell, *ed.* J L Waltman. Texas Univ. (Austin) PhD thesis, 1976. 508ff. [American food and travel writer, diary covers 1884–91.]

179. *1885* MACKENNY, HELEN G. A City Road diary: the record of three years in London, 1885–88, *ed.* A Binney and JA Vickers. Bognor Regis, Sussex: World Methodist Hist. Soc. (UK), 1978. viii, 111pp., illus.

180. *1886* BAILEY, S K *(ed.).* JOHN BAILEY, 1864–1931: letters and diaries. Murray, 1935. 325pp. [Literary critic. Contains extracts from his diary, 1886–1930.]

181. *1886* ESSERY, FLORENCE. Florence Essery's London diary, 1886–89, *ed.* J Dyer. Minerva, 1997. x, 170pp., illus.

182. *1887* GISSING, GEORGE ROBERT. London and the life of literature in late Victorian England: the diary of George Gissing, novelist, *ed.* P Coustillas. Hassocks, Sussex: Harvester P.,1978. vii, 617pp., illus. [1887–1902.]

183. *1887* LASCELLES, *Sir* ALAN. End of an era: letters and journals of Sir Alan Lascelles, *ed.* D Hart-Davis. Hamilton, 1986. [Private Secretary to George VI.]

184. *1888* BERKELEY, MAUD. Maud: the diaries of Maud Berkeley, *ed.* F Fraser. Secker, 1985. 192pp., illus. [London and Isle of Wight, 1888–1904.]

185. *1890* GARNETT, OLIVE. Tea and anarchy! The Bloomsbury diary of Olive Garnett, 1890–93. Olive and Stepniak: the Bloomsbury diary of Olive Garnett, 1893–95, *ed.* B C Johnson. Birmingham: Bartletts P., 1989, 1993. 2 vols.

186. *1895* MONKSWELL, MARY. A Victorian diarist: later extracts from the journals of Mary, Lady Monkswell, 1895–1909, *ed.* E C F Collier. Murray, 1946. 231pp., illus. [Her husband was Chairman of the LCC, 1903–04. They lived in Chelsea.]

187. *1895* NEWBURY, ARTHUR. The diary of Arthur Newbury, *ed.* D G Jackson. Congleton, Cheshire: the editor, 1997. 115pp., illus. [A footman. Covers 1895, 1898 and 1900.]

188. *1896* BENNETT, ARNOLD. The journals of Arnold Bennett, *ed.* F Swinnerton. Penguin, 1971. 599pp. [Novelist. The diaries cover 1896–1929.]

189. *1897* WOOLF, VIRGINIA. A passionate apprentice: the early journals, 1897–1907, *ed.* M A Leaska. Chatto, 1990. xlv, 444pp., illus. [Writer, Bloomsbury Group member.]

190. *1911* INGE, WILLIAM RALPH. Diary of a dean: St Paul's, 1911–34. Hutchinson, 1950. 228pp., illus.

191. *1911* LOWNDES, MARIE BELLOC. Diaries and letters, 1911–47, *ed.* S Lowndes. Chatto, 1971. xi, 291pp., illus. [Writer. Lived in Wimbledon, and Westminster.]

192. *1911* WAUGH, EVELYN. The diaries of Evelyn Waugh, *ed.* M Davie. Weidenfeld, 1976. 813pp., illus. [The novelist's diaries cover 1911–65.]

193. *1912* JONES, WALTER HENRY, and JONES, ANNETTE. Tender grace: Wapping letters and diaries, 1913–15. Vol.2, Diary of the year as mayor of Stepney, 1912–13. Vol.3, Wapping-Brighton letters. *Ed.* M Darby. Colchester, Essex: Hist. of Wapping Trust, Connor & Butler, 1992, 1994. 2 vols., illus.

194. *1913* BRITTAIN, VERA. Chronicle of youth, 1913–17, *ed.* A Bishop and T Smart. Fontana, 1981. 476pp. Wartime chronicle: diary, 1939–45, *ed.*. A Bishop and Y A Bennett. Gollancz, 1989. 352pp., illus. [Writer.]

195. *1914* MILES, HALLIE EUSTACE. Untold tales of wartime London: a personal diary. Cecil Palmer, 1930. 173pp.

196. *1914* MACDONAGH, MICHAEL. In London during the Great War: the diary of a journalist. Eyre & Spottiswoode, 1935. xvi, 336pp.

197. *1915* ASQUITH, *Lady* CYNTHIA. The diaries of Lady Cynthia Asquith, 1915–18. Century, 1968. xix, 529pp.

198. *1918* DALTON, HUGH. The political diary of Hugh Dalton, 1918–40, 1945–60, *ed.* B Pimlott. Cape, with LSE, 1986. 737pp., illus.

199. *1922* ALLENDALE, JOHN. Sailorman between the wars: being the journal of a Thames, Medway and coastal bargeman. Rochester, Kent: Hallewell, 1978. xii, 205pp., illus. [1922–39.]

200. *1924* HIBBERD, STUART. 'This – is London...' Macdonald, 1950. 322pp., illus. [BBC announcer's diary, 1924–49.]

201. *1925* MAUNG MAUNG, U. London diary. Rangoon: Burma Pubrs., 1952. 72pp. [Burmese diplomat.]

202. *1930* NICOLSON, HAROLD. Diaries and letters, 1930–39, 1939–45, 1945–62. Collins, 1966–68. 3 vols. [Politician, diplomat, journalist.]

203. *1939* VAUGHAN, KEITH. Journals, 1939–77. Murray, 1989. xviii, 217pp. [Artist.]

204. *1934* CHANNON, *Sir* HENRY. Chips: the diaries of Sir Henry Channon, *ed.* R R James. Weidenfeld, 1967. 495pp., illus. [MP. Covers 1934–58.]

205. *1936* DUGDALE, BLANCHE. Baffy: the diaries of Blanche Dugdale, 1936–47. Vallentine Mitchell, 1973. xxiv, 262pp., illus. [Active in Zionist Organisation.]

206. *1937* RITCHIE, CHARLES. The siren years: undiplomatic diaries, 1937–45. Macmillan, 1974. 216pp. [Canadian diplomat.]

207. *1938* BEARDMORE, GEORGE. Civilians at war: journals, 1938–46. Murray, 1984. 203pp., illus. [Harrow and central London.]

208. *1938* CADOGAN, *Sir* ALEXANDER. The diaries, 1938–45, *ed.* D Dilks. Cassell, 1971. 881pp., illus. [Permanent Under-Secretary, Foreign Office.]

209. *1939* BARKER, SYBIL. Sybil Barker's war: the wartime diary of a Director of Music and organist at the Royal Holloway College, *ed.* L Pike. Woking, Surrey: Churchman, 1989. ix, 84pp., illus.

210. *1939* COLVILLE, *Sir* JOHN. The fringes of power: Downing Street diaries, 1939–45. Hodder, 1985. 796pp., illus. [Assistant Private Secretary to Chamberlain and Churchill, and RAFVR pilot.]

211. *1939* FYFE, HAMILTON. Britain's wartime revolution. Gollancz, 1944. 248pp., illus. [Diary, Sept. 1939–Dec. 1942.]

212. *1939* PARTRIDGE, FRANCES. Diaries, 1939–72. Phoenix, 2001. 715pp., illus. Ups and downs: diaries, 1972–75. Weidenfeld, 2001. 361pp., illus. [Associate of the Bloomsbury group.]

213. *1939* TIMOLEON *[pseud.] i.e.* DARLING, *Sir* WILLIAM. King's Cross to Waverley. Glasgow: Hodge, 1944. 168pp. [Wartime Civil Servant's 'discursive diary'.]

214. *1939* WEYMOUTH, ANTHONY. Journal of the war years and one year later. Worcester: Littlebury, 1948. 2 vols. [BBC producer, and Harley Street specialist.]

215. *1940* BENN, TONY. Years of hope: diaries, letters and papers, 1940–62, *ed.* R Winstone. Hutchinson, 1994. xvi, 442pp., illus. Diaries, 1963–90. Hutchinson, 1988–92. 5 vols., illus. [Politician.]

216. *1940* LEE, RAYMOND E. The London observer: the journal of General Raymond E Lee, 1940–41, *ed.* J Leutze. Hutchinson, 1972. xxi, 489pp. [First pubd. Boston, Mass.: Little, Brown, 1971.]

217. *1940* NIXON, BARBARA. Raiders overhead: a diary of the London Blitz. Scolar, Gulliver, 1980. 176pp., illus. [She was an air raid warden. First pubd. Lindsay Drummond, 1943.]

218. *1940* PERRY, COLIN. Boy in the Blitz: the 1940 diary of Colin Perry. Farnham Common, Surrey: the author, 1980. 222pp., illus.

219. *1940* REYNOLDS, QUENTIN J. A London diary. New York: Angus & Robertson, 1941. 249pp. [Journalist. Originally pubd. New York: Random House, 1941.]

220. *1940* ROYDE-SMITH, NAOMI. Outside information: a diary of rumours. Macmillan, 1941. vii, 190pp. [Diaries, Sept–Oct 1940.]

221. *1941* COWARD, *Sir* NOEL. The Noel Coward diaries, *ed.* G Payn and S Morley. Weidenfeld, 1982. 698pp. [Playwright, actor. The diaries cover 1941–69.]

222. *1941* GRAVES, CHARLES P R. Off the record. A Londoner's life. Great days. Pride of the morning. Hutchinson, 1941–45. 4 vols. [Writer's wartime diaries.]

223. *1941* MENZIES, *Sir* ROBERT. Dark and hurrying days, *ed.* A W Martin and P Hardy. Canberra: National Lib. Australia, 1993. 187pp. [1941 diaries of Australian Prime Minister, covering visit to England.]

224. *1942* LEES-MILNE, JAMES. Ancestral voices. Faber, 1975. x, 301pp. Prophesying peace. Faber, 1977. 253pp. Caves of ice. Faber, 1983. 276pp. Midway on the waves. Faber, 1985. 248pp. Ancient as the hills. Murray, 1997. x, 228pp. Through wood and dale. Murray, 1998. viii, 325pp. Holy dread, *ed.* M Bloch. Murray, 2001. 240pp.

225. *1942* WILLIAMS, KENNETH. The Kenneth Williams diaries, *ed.* R Davies. Harper Collins, 1993. xxix, 827pp., illus. [Actor and comedian. Diaries cover 1942–88.]

226. *1944* BAKER, RICHARD B. The year of the buzz bomb: a journal of London, 1944. New York: Exposition, 1952. 118pp.

227. *1944* CARANDINI ALBERTINI, ELENA. Passata la stagione: diari, 1944–47. Florence: Passigli, 1989. 379pp., illus. [Italian diplomat's wife.]

228. *1946* PYM, BARBARA. A very private eye: the diaries, letters and note-books of Barbara Pym, *ed.* H Holt and H Pym. Macmillan, 1984. xvi, 358pp. [The novelist worked in London from 1946–72.]

229. *1948* ACKERLEY, J R. My sister and myself: the diaries of J R Ackerley, *ed.* F King. Hutchinson, 1982. 216pp., illus. [Literary journalist. The diaries cover 1948–59.]

230. *1964* CASTLE, *Dame* BARBARA. The Castle diaries, 1964–76. Papermac, 1990. 560pp. [Cabinet minister.]

231. *1964* CROSSMAN, RICHARD. The Crossman diaries, 1964–70, *ed.* A Howard. Hamilton, 1979. 688pp., illus. [Cabinet minister.]

232. *1965* KING, CECIL. The Cecil King diary, 1965–70; 1970–74. Cape, 1971,1975. 2 vols. [Newspaper magnate. The diaries run from 1965–74.]

233. *1966* ORTON, JOE. The Orton diaries, *ed.* J Lahr. Methuen, 1986. 304pp., illus. [Playwright. The diary covers 1966–67.]

234. *1967* STRONG, *Sir* ROY. The Roy Strong diaries, 1967–87. Weidenfeld, 1997. 462pp., illus. [Museum director, garden expert.]

235. *1974* CLARK, ALAN. Diaries: Into politics [1974–83]. In power [1983–91]. Weidenfeld, 2000, 1993. 2 vols. [Politician and bon viveur.]

236. *1974* CLARK, OSSIE. The Ossie Clark diaries, *ed.* H Rous. Bloomsbury, 1998. 453pp., illus. [Fashion designer. The diaries cover 1974–96.]

237. *1975* MARTIN, PAUL. Paul Martin: the London diaries, 1975–79, *ed.* W R Young. Ottawa: Ottawa UP, 1988. xxiii, 622pp., illus. [Canadian diplomat.]

238. *1976* BEESON, TREVOR. Window on Westminster: a canon's diary, 1976–87. SCM Press, 1998. xii,324pp., illus. [Canon of Westminster Abbey.]

239. *1978* RADJI, PARVIZ C. In the service of the Peacock Throne: the diaries of the Shah's last ambassador to London. Hamilton, 1983. 343pp., illus.

240. *1980* CASSON, *Sir* HUGH. Diary. Macmillan, 1981. 174pp., illus. [Architect. Diary of year as President of the Royal Academy, 1980.]

241. *1982* POWELL, ANTHONY. Journals, 1982–86; 1987–89; 1990–92. Heinemann, 1995–98. 3 vols. [Novelist with elevated social connections.]

242. *1985* WYATT, WOODROW. The journals of Woodrow Wyatt, *ed.* S Curtis. Macmillan, 1998, 1999. 2 vols. [1985–97. Politician and journalist.]

243. *1988* ASHDOWN, PADDY. The Ashdown diaries. Vol. 1, 1988–97. Vol. 2, 1997–99. Allen Lane, 2000, 2001. 2 vols. [Leader of the Liberal Democrats.]

244. *1990* BRANDRETH, GYLES. Breaking the code: Westminster diaries, May 1990 to May 1997. Weidenfeld, 1999. xv, 527pp., illus. [Politician, media personality.]

INDEX TO THE BIBLIOGRAPHY:
DIARISTS, EDITORS AND
AUTHORS

LONDON RECORD SOCIETY

President: The Rt. Hon. the Lord Mayor of London

Chairman: H.S.Cobb, MA, FSA, FRHS
Hon. Secretary: H.J.Creaton, BA, MPhil, ALA
Hon. Treasurer: G.Pick
Hon. General Editors: V.A.Harding, MA, PhD, FRHS
S.O'Connor, BA, PhD

The London Record Society was founded in December 1964 to publish transcripts, abstracts and lists of the primary sources for the history of London, and generally to stimulate interest in archives relating to London. Membership is open to any individual or institution; the annual subscription is £12 (US $22) for individuals and £18 (US $35) for institutions. Prospective members should apply to the Hon. Secretary, Miss H.J.Creaton, c/o Institute of Historical Research, Senate House, London WC1E 7HU.

The following volumes have already been published:
1. *London Possessory Assizes: a calendar*, edited by Helena M. Chew (1965)
2. *London Inhabitants within the Walls, 1695*, with an introduction by D.V.Glass (1966)
3. *London Consistory Court Wills, 1492–1547*, edited by Ida Darlington (1967)
4. *Scriveners' Company Common Paper, 1357–1628, with a continuation to 1678*, edited by Francis W. Steer (1968)
5. *London Radicalism, 1830–1843: a selection from the papers of Francis Place*, edited by D. J. Rowe (1970)
6. *The London Eyre of 1244*, edited by Helena M. Chew and Martin Weinbaum (1970)
7. *The Cartulary of Holy Trinity Aldgate*, edited by Gerald A. J. Hodgett (1971)
8. *The Port and Trade of early Elizabethan London: Documents*, edited by Brian Dietz (1972)
9. *The Spanish Company*, edited by Pauline Croft (1973)
10. *London Assize of Nuisance, 1301–1431: a calendar*, edited by Helena M. Chew and William Kellaway (1973)
11. *Two Calvinistic Methodist Chapels, 1748–1811: the London Tabernacle and Spa Fields Chapel*, edited by Edwin Welch (1975)
12. *The London Eyre of 1276*, edited by Martin Weinbaum (1976)
13. *The Church in London, 1375–1392*, edited by A. K. McHardy (1977)
14. *Committees for the Repeal of the Test and Corporation Acts: Minutes, 1786–90 and 1827–8*, edited by Thomas W. Davis (1978)

15. *Joshua Johnson's Letterbook, 1771–4: letters from a merchant in London to his partners in Maryland*, edited by Jacob M. Price (1979)

16. *London and Middlesex Chantry Certificate, 1548*, edited by C. J. Kitching (1980)

17. *London Politics, 1713–1717: Minutes of a Whig Club, 1714–17*, edited by H.Horwitz; *London Pollbooks, 1713*, edited by W.A. Speck and W.A. Gray (1981)

18. *Parish Fraternity Register: Fraternity of the Holy Trinity and SS.Fabian and Sebastian in the parish of St. Botolph without Aldersgate*, edited by Patricia Basing (1982)

19. *Trinity House of Deptford: Transactions, 1609–35*, edited by G.G.Harris (1983)

20. *Chamber Accounts of the sixteenth century*, edited by Betty R. Masters (1984)

21. *The Letters of John Paige, London Merchant, 1648–58*, edited by George F. Steckley (1984)

22. *A Survey of Documentary Sources for Property Holding in London before the Great Fire*, by Derek Keene and Vanessa Harding (1985)

23. *The Commissions for Building Fifty New Churches*, edited by M.H.Port (1986)

24. *Richard Hutton's Complaints Book*, edited by Timothy V. Hitchcock (1987)

25. *Westminster Abbey Charters, 1066–c. 1214*, edited by Emma Mason (1988)

26. *London Viewers and their Certificates, 1508–1558*, edited by Janet S. Loengard (1989)

27. *The Overseas Trade of London: Exchequer Customs Accounts, 1480–1*, edited by H.S.Cobb (1990)

28. *Justice in Eighteenth-century Hackney: the Justicing Notebook of Henry Norris and the Hackney Petty Sessions Book*, edited by Ruth Paley (1991)

29. *Two Tudor Subsidy Assessment Rolls for the City of London: 1541 and 1582*, edited by R.G.Lang (1993)

30. *London Debating Societies, 1776–1799*, compiled and introduced by Donna T. Andrew (1994)

31. *London Bridge: selected accounts and rentals, 1381–1538*, edited by Vanessa Harding and Laura Wright (1995)

32. *London Consistory Court Depositions, 1586–1611: list and indexes*, by Loreen L.Giese (1997)

33. *Chelsea settlement and bastardy examinations, 1733–66*, edited by Tim Hitchcock and John Black (1999)

34. *The church records of St Andrew Hubbard Eastcheap, c. 1450–c. 1570*, edited by Clive Burgess (1999)

35. *Calendar of Exchequer Equity pleadings, 1685–6 and 1784–5*, edited by Henry Horwitz and Jessica Cooke (2000)

36. *The Letters of William Freeman, London Merchant, 1678–1685*, edited by David Hancock (2002)

37. *Unpublished London diaries. A checklist of unpublished diaries by Londoners and visitors, with a select bibliography of published diaries*, compiled by Heather Creaton (2003)

Most volumes are still in print; apply to the Hon. Secretary, who will forward requests to the distributor. Price to individual members £12 ($22) each, to non-members £20 ($38) each.